FROM GRIEF
TO GLORY

FROM GRIEF TO GLORY

The Rise of the Centurion

ERIC A. LOMAX

Trilogy Christian Publishers A Wholly Owned Subsidiary of Trinity Broadcasting Network 2442 Michelle Drive Tustin, CA 92780

Trilogy Christian Publishing/ TBN and colophon are trademarks of Trinity Broadcasting Network.

For information about special discounts for bulk purchases, please contact Trilogy Christian Publishing.

Trilogy Disclaimer: The views and content expressed in this book are those of the author and may not necessarily reflect the views and doctrine of Trilogy Christian Publishing or the Trinity Broadcasting Network.

Manufactured in the United States of America

10 9 8 7 6 5 4 3 2 1

Library of Congress Cataloging-in-Publication Data is available.

ISBN#: 978-1-64773-162-5

E-ISBN#: 978-1-64773-163-2

DEDICATION

My beloved Kenisha, may you rest in peace, knowing that our love will always be eternal and infinite. The memories of our journey and all that we shared will be treasured in my heart until the day comes that we can be together again. Nothing could have prepared me for the task of losing you, but I thank God for the wonderful years that we had together.

Thank you for being my wife, friend, and rock through everything. Thank you for loving Tristan and treating her like she was your own flesh and blood. Now I will seek to honor your memory with this book as I carry out the will of God for my life. Death will never be victorious over our love, nor will it ever separate us. Until then, I will keep you in that special place within my heart where only you can reside. I love you, Pooter.

Acknowledgments

I would like to give special thanks to Pastor Gerald Johnson for helping me to know and understand that the sun would shine again. Your heartfelt words helped me to make it through the darkness and fog. I now stand in the confidence of the light, and I am ready to journey on.

Although I have never met Pastor Joel Osteen, I would like to thank him for his obedience to doing the will of God. Thank you for the numerous messages that brought me back from the darkness and despair. Your words kept me and allowed me to know and understand that God still cares for me.

Pastor Tricia P. Jamerson was a true inspiration over the years. She is better known as the "Purpose Doula," and she helped me to birth this work. Tricia, your prayers and words of encouragement were immeasurable. Thanks for all of those wonderful breakfast strategy meetings.

Pastor Bob Shirock is a true gift from God. I didn't know it at the time, but God led me to you for the healing I so desperately needed. Thank you for helping me to understand the God-sized hole within my heart and how to overcome the pain of loss.

TABLE OF CONTENTS

LOVE STORY

I was a year out of my divorce from my second wife and was just trying to find my way again. I felt like a failure and that marriage may not have been in the cards for me since I did not expect to face divorce yet again. In my mind, I cringed at the thought of being married for a third time, but deep down inside, I had hoped that one day, I would find true love. The only bright spot from my second marriage was my beautiful daughter, Tristan Noelle. She was my pride and joy, and I was so enamored with this little bundle of joy from the moment she was born.

My divorce was still a sore spot in my mind because we had no grounds for it, other than the fact that my ex-wife just didn't want to be with me anymore. However, I was done with the constant bickering and endless counseling sessions that produced nothing. The only thing that really mattered was Tristan and how this would affect her.

I knew that the relationship between a father and a daughter was special. A daughter should receive as much love as possible from her father because this will be her first impression of a man. So I made up in my mind that no matter what happened between me and Tori, I would always be there for her.

I was also driven by the fact that my first marriage had produced a son that was deeply scarred by the divorce. His mother did not want him, and she signed custody over to me. He always longed for his mother's love, and at times, he would do reckless acts in school to get me frustrated enough to send him to her. I would always oblige his request because I wanted him to be happy. On every occasion, I would call his mother and tell her that he wanted to be with her, and she would always give in to the request. However, in a few weeks, she would always call me in frustration, stating that she couldn't deal with him.

He came back to me every time, wondering why his mother didn't want him. I tried to do my best to help him, but I was not equipped to handle what was going through his mind at the time. My son and I went to counseling sessions but to no avail because Evan wouldn't let go of the anger that he felt. He channeled this anger against me and his family here in Detroit. He blamed us for all his problems and held his mother in a saintly position.

With my second divorce, I was determined not to have this history repeat itself with my daughter. I swore to God and everyone else that I would be the best father possible. I was not going to let anyone, not even Tori, stop me from being in Tristan's life. She was much too precious for that to happen.

We had a special bond between us. When she was born, I was the first one to bond with her. Tori had to deliver her by C-section because Tristan was not coming down the birth canal, and the doctors were afraid that she would lose precious oxygen. I was in the operating room with her as they performed the procedure. When the doctor took the baby from the womb, the nurses took her over to another area in the room. I stood close watch over them as they took our babies vital signs. At the same time, I was talking to Tori across the room, telling her how beautiful our baby was.

After the nurses finished checking our baby, I leaned over her and began to talk to her. As her eyes locked on to the sound of my voice, I noticed that she wasn't crying. She looked at me as if she had known me before. But I think she recognized my voice because I talked to my wife's stomach almost every day.

Tristan started to make this little cooing noise as I spoke to her, and then she smiled. At that point, I was overcome with tears. I think Tristan knew she had me in the palm of her hand. Her hold on my heart has continued to this day. There is nothing that I wouldn't do for Tristan. I used to tell her all the time that I would always be there for her. If she went to the moon, then Daddy would go to the moon.

The church that Tori and I had been attending tried to help us stay together, but my soon-to-be ex-wife had successfully managed to make me look like a monster in the eyes of the pastor. She had this uncanny ability to make people think she was an angel, but only I knew the truth about her. I'm not saying that I was without fault as it takes two to tango. But let's just say that Tori brought her own issues to the destruction of our marriage.

Tori really played the role of the victim to the tee, and she succeeded in making the pastor cast judgement upon me. After the divorce, I stayed at the church in hopes of redeeming myself and showing leadership that I wasn't the boogeyman. Tori tried to stick around, but she soon left the church. I thought this would have vindicated me, but it did little to sway the opinions of those who stood in judgment over me.

I decided to meet with the pastor to see if we could discuss ways that I could serve in the ministry. After all, I was still an ordained minister, despite my setbacks. I foolishly thought I could be of service to the church and possibly help others that were struggling with marital issues.

On the day of our meeting, I was excited to sit down and talk to the man I thought was praying for me, but a few minutes into the meeting, I discovered the truth. He totally disrespected me and questioned my ministerial credentials. I was sitting there in complete shock as he went on a rant about my character and the fact that I was a divorced man. In short, he told me that I had no place in his church.

At this point, I ended the meeting and thanked him for his time. I left his office, feeling confused and let down, but I continued to attend the services. I don't know why. Maybe I was trying to prove something to him or to myself. After a few weeks of sitting there in the pew and receiving no support, I decided to leave the church because the rumors and gossip were too much to endure.

I wasn't sure of where I was going. I had the option of going back to my former church, Glad Tidings COGIC, which is where Tori and I were married. We left that church in an attempt to save our marriage. As I thought about it, going back did not seem right at the time. Truthfully, I really did not think that Glad Tidings would receive me again. Most of the people I had known stopped talking to me after we left. I did not want to be hasty about my decision. I had been taught throughout my time in ministry it was best to put all things before God in prayer and allow Him to direct my steps. So I waited for his answer and direction concerning my next move. I was confident that He would lead me because He had guided me through several ministerial transitions in the past.

One night, I was coming home from work and was hungry. I decided to stop at this restaurant along my route and get a carryout order. When I walked in the door, I was met by Pastor Faulk. Pastor Faulk had often visited the church that I was preparing to leave. He gave me a big hug and a smile as we stood, waiting for our food. Pastor Faulk asked me about the church, and I told him of my decision to seek another church, and I was waiting for God to direct me. He seemed concerned and excited at the same time.

As I tried to figure out his reaction to my news, he started to tell me that he was opening a church of his own, and I should attend the next Sunday. He also went on to tell me he was searching for ministerial help because he wanted to make sure the church would grow. I told him I was ordained and that I would like to attend to see if I could be of service to him. He was so excited as he gave me the address and the time service would start.

I was excited and amazed at how God had engineered this encounter because I would have normally gone home and made a sandwich. But on this night, I had the strong urge to stop at this restaurant. As I drove home, I pondered whether this was God directing me or if it was just a coincidence. In any case, I decided to attend the service the following Sunday.

When the day came, I entered the church and was greeted by a host of men and women. They were all so warm and inviting. I could tell this was my next church home. I was excited at the chance to serve and be a part of the growth of this ministry. When the pastor came out, he looked at me and smiled. He then motioned for me to come and sit in the pulpit with him. I am not one to make a spectacle, but I could sense the congregants were wondering who I was. When the pastor got up to address them, he introduced me and told them of my credentials and how he believed God had directed our providential meeting.

The members clapped and praised God while smiling in approval. It was all so overwhelming and heartwarming at the same time. I had finally found a place to serve, and I was eager to help in any way I could.

After joining the church, I was immediately put to work. I opened service, taught Sunday School, and would occasionally be called to preach a sermon. I was soon named the superintendent of the Sunday School, which was a great honor because it gave me a chance to teach. I enjoyed teaching more than anything, and I often looked forward to studying the lessons.

Over the years, the ministry grew, and we installed other associate ministers to assist in the work. We were all deeply engaged, and all things were solid. I was getting through the healing process of my divorce, and I was starting to date.

Dating was not the greatest because I was meeting so many women who did not meet my requirements. I only had a couple of what I call non-negotiables on my list. My first non-negotiable was that my future wife would have to love God more than me. I did not want a woman who did not have a strong foundation in God because I was a minister. Also, I needed someone who could walk with me and be there for me through the struggles of ministry. Ministry and serving others can be quite taxing to your physical and spiritual self, so the woman that was to be with me had to understand this fact. To be the wife of a minister was not for the faint of heart.

My only other requirement was that my future wife would have to love Tristan as much as I loved her. This was huge to me because I had heard horror stories of women who tricked men into marrying them and then caused discourse between them and their children. The women would feign interest in the child all while dating. But soon after marriage, they would turn on them. I never wanted this to happen to Tristan, and I had already been through one marriage where my wife didn't want her own child, so I knew it was possible.

I briefly dated a woman that gave up her son for adoption because she did not want to be a mother. I dropped her quickly when I found this fact out. I was so concerned with not making this mistake that I often prayed to God, asking him to send me a woman who would love my daughter like she was her own. It was important for me that my daughter was respected and loved because she was a part of me. You can't say that you love me and not love my child. I made it very clear to everyone that we were a package deal.

One day, a very beautiful lady came to visit the church. She was the sister of one of our regular members. Her name was Kenisha Doyle. I immediately took great notice of her. There was something about her that I could not seem to shake. Yes, she was beautiful, and she exuded so much grace and style. Physically, she was perfect for me, and I could not have asked for anything else. She had long hair, a nice shape, and an infectious smile that would melt the devil's heart. But all these traits were not what my thoughts were centered on.

There was something about her inner being that was calling to me whenever I saw her. It was as if I could look deep into her soul and see the wonderful beauty of the Spirit of God upon her. It was hard for me to take my eyes off her, but I was scared to say anything to her because I knew she was very young.

I noticed her every time she came into the sanctuary, and after service was over, I would go over and stand near her just to get a closer look. On some occasions, I would talk to some of her family members, hoping they would introduce me to her. She had several family members at the church, and to my knowledge, they all liked me.

One day, after Bible study, I mustered the courage to finally say something to her. I don't know why I was so nervous, but my heart was racing as I was trying to figure out what to say. I introduced myself to her as she stood there, talking to her sister, Marcenia. Marcenia smiled at me with this goofy grin and introduced me to Kenisha. This broke the ice and made it easy for us to talk. As I settled my nerves, I noticed Kenisha opened up to me without hesitation. We stood there, talking, and it seemed like we were in our own little world because everyone else seemed to disappear. She was so easy to talk to, and I really admired her spirit. Afterward, she shook my hand and gave me that heartwarming smile. From that point on, I knew I was sprung. I couldn't wait to see her again.

After a couple of weeks, Kenisha joined the church and became a regular attendee of my Sunday School class. I would always look for her because she was very in tune with my class. She asked questions, took notes, and seemed to hang on to every word I spoke. After class, she would tell me how she enjoyed the class, which made me feel good knowing that my students were gaining knowledge. But in truth, I was only concerned about her and what she thought. I would have taught her anything she wanted to know if it would give me a chance to be in her presence.

After class, she would always come up and give me that beautiful smile and ask me more questions about the lesson to which I would gladly answer. It gave me an excuse to gaze into her wondrous eyes. Also, it gave me a chance to get to know her because she was very comfortable speaking to me. On other occasions, I would often stop her in the parking lot and ask her how school was going or how her day was. She would always smile and tell me about what she was dealing with and that she was not going to give up.

Kenisha faced insurmountable obstacles in her life, but you could see the drive and determination in her to succeed. She was not going to let anything stop her in her pursuit of life and her pursuit of God. I was so amazed by her tenacity that it made me want to be better. Kenisha was young and full of fire. She far surpassed her peers and even the women that were my age. She had this wisdom about her that made it seem like she was much older than she was.

Even Pastor Faulk took notice of her and talked about her with me on some occasions. I was interested to hear how he felt about her because I respected his opinion. He asked me on numerous occasions if I was interested in anyone at the church. I told him I did not feel that any of the women were up to my standards. However, Pastor Faulk did mention a few he thought were worthy. I was not attracted to any of them since most of them looked homely and appeared boring.

My focus remained on Kenisha. She was beautiful, she had style, and she looked like she knew how to enjoy herself outside of the church. She wasn't so saved that she could not find enjoyment in other things. She loved to go to the movies, attend concerts and plays, and she loved to travel. She also enjoyed an occasional glass of wine, which I thought was perfect.

As time went on, Kenisha began to get involved in the ministry. Everyone saw the Spirit of God working in her life, and there was no doubt that she possessed Godly gifts. You could see that she had a hunger and thirst for the things of God. She was bold and not ashamed to let the world know about her past. Her testimony was touching, and I was amazed by her willingness to share with others how God had saved and freed her from a life of sin and shame.

Kenisha used to live with her boyfriend who was a local drug dealer. Her life at that time was filled with lavish things like clothes, shoes, and accessories. Money was never an issue because her boyfriend would supply her with anything she wanted. She didn't think about the consequences of jail nor the dangers of being murdered. She just went along with the lifestyle and lived carefree.

In her mind, her life was set because she had come from a rough upbringing. Her mom, Carmeta, was never married to her biological father, Kenneth. However, Carmeta did marry a man by the name of Stanley who became Kenisha's stepfather. This union produced two children: her sister, Marcenia, and her brother, Stanley Jr., who was affectionately known as Little Stan. Kenisha loved both of them very much, but Little Stan was her favorite. She often referred to him as her baby. Kenisha was the best big sister to her siblings, and she often went out of her way to provide for them.

Unfortunately, Carmeta passed away from cancer when Kenisha was sixteen years old. During this time, she managed to graduate from high school while taking care of herself. Her biological father, Kenny, was in and out of her life, and she could not depend on him for support. Kenny had married another woman and had stepchildren that he supported. At one point, I believe he tried to have Kenisha come and live with them. I am not sure why she never moved with them, but I do believe it was the result of the tense relationship between them.

Her stepfather, Stanley Sr., on the other hand, was abusive as well as a drug addict. Kenisha would often tell me of Stan's fits of rage against her mother. She described him as being very controlling and jealous. This probably didn't give Kenisha a good representation of what real men were like, but nonetheless, she still had her desire to be in a solid relationship.

Through all of this, Kenisha had to grow up in a hurry, and I believe this is where her sage wisdom was produced. She was a fighter and a go-getter. At the age of eighteen, Kenisha was working two jobs while going to school and renting her own apartment. Her drive to succeed would not be diminished, and she wouldn't let anything stand in her way. When I heard Kenisha tell her story, I was so impressed with her because most twenty-five-year-old women could not keep up with her. Her drive and determination, coupled with her wisdom, drew me closer to her.

There was something about her that really intrigued me, and I wanted to know more. But I was still unsure of pursuing her because we were so far apart in age. She was sixteen years my junior. I was afraid that we would have too many differences of opinion due to our age.

Even though I was very impressed with Kenisha, her age was a strong deterrent to my pursuit of anything with her. During this time,

I continued to date other women while trying to figure out my feelings for Kenisha. I was conflicted over my thoughts of her. As much as I tried to shake my feelings, Kenisha was always on my mind.

I wasn't having much success with finding the right woman, and I even considered going back with my ex-wife, Tori, since we had Tristan whom I dearly loved. Like I said before, my daughter was my pride and joy. I loved Tristan more than anything in this world. She had me wrapped around her finger from day one, and she was the only reason why I would consider going back to Tori.

I had been going along in life just fine, but there was a moment I did reconsider our marriage. My ex-wife was coming around more often, and there was still a small spark there for her. So we began to try to work things out. We went out on a few dates, and I would go over to Tori's place and spend time with her and Tristan. It was starting to feel like a family relationship again, but I knew we had some obstacles to overcome. One of the huge hurdles was her mother, Diane, and the fact she did not like me. Truthfully, I was not a fan of her mother, but I tolerated her.

One day, Tori and I met with Pastor Faulk for counseling, and he listened to our issues and offered his advice. He wanted me to apologize to Diane, even though I did nothing wrong. I considered it and was a little hesitant, but if it meant that we could reconcile, I was willing to try. Pastor Faulk wanted me to take Diane out to dinner where we could sit and talk. Tori could not be present because Pastor Faulk wanted us to air our grievances to one another without any interference.

Tori balked at the suggestion, but she later relented. Without going into detail, the entire encounter was a disaster. I tried to remain humble as Diane railed against me and my treatment of her and Tori. We ended the evening with nothing accomplished, but I did tell Diane that I was going to pursue reconciliation, regardless of her feelings toward me.

A few weeks after the encounter with Diane, Tori came to me and said she was pregnant and that I was going to be a father again. Yes, we were sleeping together during this time. I had no reason to question it. I really didn't know how to feel about it, but I thought it was the deciding force in keeping us together. However, I would soon come to find out that Tori was not being truthful with me. Another man named Ralph had surfaced, and it was at that point I began to feel the unborn baby was not mine.

Tori tried to convince me, but it didn't help. The other man was calling me and detailing their sexual exploits and all the times that she traveled to see him. He lived in Pennsylvania, which was a nine-hour drive from Detroit. At this point, I was confused and not really focused on pursuing the reconciliation. I didn't know whether I should be angry with her for lying or the fact that she was having another man's baby. Plus, Ralph was calling me, constantly crying about how much she hurt him with her deception. I really didn't want to hear him and did everything in my power to stay in control of my emotions. In truth, I didn't blame him because she lied to both of us, but this guy was a true piece of work. We continued to date, but my mind was still in a state of flux.

I really don't know why I didn't end things with Tori after hearing about the other guy. I think it was because Ralph had made me so angry with his taunts. I wanted to make him suffer because I had her with me, and I knew this upset him. Maybe it was because I was not sure if the baby was mine or not. If it was, it would solidify our relationship. However, if it wasn't, it would be hard to contend with another man's child. I hung in there because I really needed to know before I made a decision.

One night, Tori and I went out and, before long, got into an argument over something stupid. This was par for the course. The argument thrust us right back into the thick of our previous marriage, and I felt the intensity of the anger boiling over. It was at this point I knew she was never going to change. We would forever be trapped in the maze of endless finger-pointing. She was always going to be right, and I was always going to be wrong. I decided to cut my losses and get out before it got worse. Who knows how things would have gone? But I do know I could not bear taking care of another man's baby. That was the ultimate humiliation. I was not going to be made to look like a fool.

On the following Sunday morning, I was sitting in the pulpit of our church, talking to God before opening the service. My mind was swirling with thoughts of betrayal and all the other past failures. My head was heavy as it sank lower and lower into my shoulders. As I murmured my prayer to God, I told Him that I was done with searching for another woman. If he wanted me to be single and follow Him, I would do my best.

I was honest with God when I told Him it might not be good for me to be single because I always managed to get into situations with women. It was never difficult for me to be with a woman. I knew that I had a certain charm with the ladies. Some people thought it was my green eyes that made women swoon, but that was only part of the allure.

I have always been able to talk to women, and I guess they found my conversation intoxicating. I have never had any problems with conversations. I love to talk and I love to use words to invoke feelings. My enticing words flow naturally without thought or hesitation. It was this charm that always got me into trouble. It was good trouble, but I wanted to be different. I wanted to try to be celibate, but that word was not in my vocabulary. Even when I tried, I would run into a female who could not control herself around me. Pretty soon, we were in the sheets, and I was looking up to God and shaking my head. I never tried to lie to God because I figured if I was truthful about myself, He would help me to overcome my temptations. So as I sat in the pulpit, I told God I could not make Him any promises. But I would try to stay away from women.

Suddenly, I heard a voice as clear as day speaking to me. I knew it was the voice of God because there was no one else around me. I was the only one sitting in the pulpit at the time. As I listened, I heard His voice say to me, "I'm glad that you have given up looking because your wife is right there." I looked up in front of me and noticed two women standing in one of the rows talking. As I stared at them, I became depressed since I was not attracted to neither one of them. I spoke back to God, asking Him, "Is this my punishment for my past sins? I told You that I wanted to be completely honest. If this is the case, then I would rather be alone. It doesn't make sense to be with someone who I am not attracted to." Women need to understand that men are visual creatures, and we are attracted to them by what we see. If the package is not pleasing to the eye, we will keep moving on.

Those two women could not have held my interest for one second. As I mounted my opposition to the voice, it began to speak again, and in a soft whisper, it told me to look again. My focus seemed to sharpen like a microscope peering into the cellular world. The two women began to fade as my eyesight became fixated on a woman sitting behind them. This woman was angelic in her grace and beauty. Immediately, I began to gaze at her sitting there, and I noticed she had all the physical qualities that I wanted. I began to sense a joy come over me, and I could feel my heart swelling because the voice was confirming that she was my future. This beautiful lady's name was Kenisha Doyle, and she was drop-dead gorgeous!

Kenisha was beautiful and smart. But I was still concerned with our age difference. Sixteen years was a huge gap in my mind, and I wondered if we could be compatible. I also thought that she would never be attracted to me. She would probably look at me like I was some dirty, perverted old man.

Was I really hearing from God? Or was I just making this all up in my head? Even before this moment of confirmation, I had noticed her when she first came to visit the church, and I knew that I was attracted to her. But I was scared she would reject me or she would tell me she was involved with someone else. Either way, I would still end up looking like a fool for going after a younger lady who was not much older than my son.

I sat in that pulpit and wrestled with my thoughts. I was ready to dismiss this crazy notion of her being my wife when the voice spoke again. I wish I could tell you that the heavens opened and the angels descended upon me, singing hymns of praise. No, all I heard was, "Just wait and see."

Over the next few weeks, I couldn't help but notice her. Every time she walked into the sanctuary, my eyes locked onto her. Kenisha moved with the grace of an angel, and her smile was soft and warm. Her beauty radiated both inside and out, and I could not deny wanting to be in her presence. People were drawn to Kenisha like a moth to a flame. She always had someone around her wanting to talk with her or just to be in her presence.

The one thing I noticed most about her was she was hardworking and was focused on her goals. Determination was woven throughout her DNA, and Kenisha wasn't going to let anything stand in her way. If you looked up the word *diligent*, her image would have been right next to the meaning of the word. I would see her after church and ask her how she was doing. She would always tell me that she was working hard to get her life together because she wanted the best that life had to offer. In those brief conversations, I would encourage her to keep striving for what she wanted because it would work itself out in the end. I wanted to encourage her to be her best because I could see she wanted nothing less.

She possessed the same tenacity in her spiritual walk with God. You could tell she was serious about serving God and learning more about Him. We would see each other in the parking lot after service, and she would always ask me questions about certain scriptures. I was always willing to talk with her, so I really looked forward to our parking lot encounters. During those moments, I got a chance to really see what she was all about. I could tell that she was serious, and this tenacity made me want her more and more.

Kenisha was hungry and thirsty for the knowledge of God. I could see the Spirit of God in her molding and shaping her into this lovely vessel. At one point, I paused to consider whether I could be worthy of walking alongside her as a husband because her power was undeniable. Many church members saw what I saw and said that she was going to do great things for God. My attraction to her was growing stronger and stronger each day, and I could not get her out of my mind. I felt this deep spiritual connection to Kenisha that I had never felt before. I could feel her presence whenever she wasn't around me.

On Sunday mornings, before getting up to open the service, I would feel thoughts of Kenisha in my spirit. In a few moments, she would walk through the doors, looking like a true vision of loveliness. This always brought a smile to my face, and I became aware that I was falling in love with her. The voice of God was confirming that we were meant to be together, and soon it was confirmed by the Holy Spirit. I didn't know it at the time, but God was knitting our souls together.

I wanted to continue with my observations a while longer before revealing my true intentions to her. I was still hesitant to put myself out there for everyone to see. I guess I was more concerned about what others would think. However, I am glad that I did wait because one of my fears was confirmed on one Sunday morning. She entered the church as usual, but I noticed that she had someone with her this time. As she went to her seat, I noticed a man walking with her. As they sat down, I noticed that he had this big, self-confident smile on his face.

My first thought was, *Who is this wolf that has come into the sanctuary?* My attention stayed on him the entire time, and I knew in my heart that I disliked him. This may seem odd because I didn't know him nor had I ever met him. But there was something about him that was fake to me. His motives appeared to be transparent. My inner gut feeling was not good; however, I played it cool.

After church, she brought him up to meet the pastor. I stayed in the background, observing them while I was talking to some other friends. I could tell that this guy was not right. He had the signs of deception written over that slick wily grin on his face. My spirit was screaming on the inside! I didn't like the situation at all. My instinct to strike him had to be subverted as it would have been bad if I had reacted the way I was feeling. I literally wanted to pick him up and throw him out of the church. Who did he think he was fooling? As we used to say in the streets, "Game recognize game." Pastor Faulk wasn't persuaded by him as well because we talked after they left. So my instincts were confirmed.

The next Sunday, after service was over, I asked Kenisha about the guy she was with. Kenisha began to tell me that they had been dating a couple of months, but she wasn't sure about him. Without any hesitation, I boldly told her that he was not the one for her. After I said this, the look on her face was one of pure astonishment, but Kenisha did not protest what I said. I knew she wanted to hear what I had to say. So I told her that I got the impression he was not true and that he was hiding something. I couldn't put my finger on it, but I knew he was a wolf and that she needed to be careful with him. I was even shocked with my words because I went on about this guy, and I had never met him before. However, my discernment had never led me wrong, and I have learned to trust the Spirit of God.

Afterward, she thanked me for my opinion and promised to be on guard. I told her that I would pray that God would reveal his true motives to her. This appeared to give Kenisha a sense of relief to know that I was looking out for her. I knew I had finally gained her trust by her reaction to everything I said as she was smiling all the time that we were talking. My judgment of the situation gave her pause as she didn't want to give in to the wrong man. I told her that I would always watch out for her because I felt that we had gotten closer to one another in our conversations. I really wanted her to be careful because I knew at that point, she was desiring a husband.

I reminded her that the counterfeit always comes before the truth. It will always seek to hinder and distract the plan of God. When I said this, a look of amazement came over her face. It was as if I had given her the confirmation that she was seeking.

Kenisha thanked me again and told me she was going to fast and pray for the answer. From that day on, I never saw her friend again. A few weeks later, she came to me and said she had ended her relationship with him because it wasn't right. She had noticed some things about him that didn't add up. In any case, it was over, and I was smiling on the inside.

My final confirmation came during a Wednesday night Bible study class. As usual, I opened the service with testimonies from the members and prayer. I was moved to anoint everyone with oil before praying, but after searching everywhere in the pulpit, there was no oil to be found. Now, any other time, there would have been several bottles to choose from; but on this night, not a single drop.

When I announced to the congregation that I didn't have any anointing oil, Kenisha stood up and said that she had a bottle of oil in her purse. As she walked up to hand it to me, I couldn't help but feel this strong attraction to her. It was at that moment that I knew Kenisha was the one that God had for me. My helpmate was standing right there before me, and I could no longer deny the fact that I wanted her in my life forever. Standing there in front of the congregation, the Holy Spirit, and God, I laid my hand on her forehead to anoint her. Our connection had been solidified in the heavens, and now it was being confirmed on earth. There was no doubt in my mind that I wanted her to be my wife, but there were a few obstacles that needed to be addressed before moving forward.

Over the next few weeks, I tried to find the best way to let Kenisha know that I wanted to pursue a lifetime with her. I was still concerned about the age gap and what people would say. My pastor seemed supportive during our conversations, but I didn't make my intentions clear to him. He wanted me to consider another woman in the church named Cheryl, who, according to him, was successful and more in my age range. There was just one problem. I was not attracted to this woman in any way. She was not my type physically or spiritually. She seemed very boring to me.

If anyone knows me, they know that boredom is a death sentence for me. If you can't keep me interested, my mind and my body will tend to wander. Kenisha had everything I wanted, and I saw life in her. So I continued to ask other people their opinions. They all said that I must be crazy because she was too young for me.

I had a very good friend of mine by the name of Beverly Edwards. She has since gone home to be with the Lord, but while she was here, she was my big sister whom I could always count on. I respected her opinion in everything because she had proven herself to be a good friend who gave wise counsel.

At first, Beverly objected to the age difference, but she told me that she wanted to meet Kenisha in person before making her final judgement. I told her no problem and that I would come visit her at her church. The following Sunday, we went to visit Beverly's church. Kenisha was dressed in a beautiful cream suit with all the appropriate accessories. She could give any first lady a run for her money because Kenisha looked like she was a pastor's wife. Our styles complimented each other very well.

As we entered the church, I was greeted by the ushers and taken to a seat a couple of rows behind Beverly. When we sat down, Beverly looked back at me and smiled. She also looked at Kenisha, and I could tell she was checking her out. My plan was to introduce Kenisha during the guest welcome, but to my surprise, a few moments later, Beverly looked back at me and smiled again. She began to mouth to me that she approved of her and that she was the one.

Wow! Kenisha didn't even have to talk to her to get her approval. She won over Beverly with her spirit. I knew Kenisha was special, and Beverly's approval meant everything to me. As far as I was concerned, I didn't need anyone else's approval or confirmation. Beverly was my deciding factor. Later, Beverly would tell me how impressed she was with the way Kenisha carried herself. She said that we looked like we belonged together. Later, Kenisha and Beverly formed a lasting bond of friendship. They often talked, and my wife always sought Beverly out for counsel on matters involving church and life.

Kenisha had a presence that was unmistakable. Wherever she went, people could not help but notice her. It was as if a herald would precede her, announcing her presence before she entered the room. I used to be in awe of her because she radiated the love of God and attracted many people to her. Kenisha carried herself like royalty, but she never looked down on anyone because she didn't consider herself to be special. Her grace, kindness, and that beautiful smile were undeniable. In fact, I think she could put the devil himself at ease with her charm. Yes, Kenisha Doyle was truly one of a kind.

The funny thing about all of this is the fact that she was an introvert. Kenisha never wanted to be in the spotlight, and her preference was to remove herself from the attention that she received. She was content with remaining in the background. This amazed me because I would always tell her that she couldn't hide. Her presence, power, and authority were too noticeable. Her spirit was like this huge star radiating in the darkness, drawing all to see the magnificence of God's glory.

What was even more amazing was that we were like night and day to each other. Kenisha was an introvert, and I was an extrovert. I have been told my personality is larger than life while Kenisha was very reserved. We balanced each other because she gave me a sense of peace. I tend to fly by the seat of my pants. Kenisha kept me grounded and helped me to make sound decisions. I truly loved that about her. She knew how to handle me and get me where I needed to be. We were a true team in every sense. It is hard to believe that even though she was sixteen years my junior, she was my equal in every way.

I have never believed in soul mates. I thought that it was some sappy cliché term, but Kenisha gave me a true understanding of the term. She was my soul mate that God prepared for me before the beginning of time.

Kenisha Doyle was the wife that I always hoped for. I had struck out on marriage twice and didn't want to make another mistake. However, I knew that she was my future and my redemption from my previous disasters. She was a great representation of the Proverbs 31 virtuous woman who made me feel powerful and respected. Her belief in me and my talents drove me to be better and pursue a higher excellence. God had answered all of my prayers when He showed me this beautiful woman. This made me want to praise Him more and more each day. My heart was thankful and full of joy whenever I thought about her.

I couldn't wait for Kenisha to be my wife. So I began to develop my plan to propose to her. At the time, I didn't have much, but I would have moved heaven and earth to get Kenisha what she deserved.

Ladies, if your man is not excited about you in every way, he is not the one for you. If he is not willing to sacrifice all for your love, he is not the one. When he looks at you, you should see the joy in his eyes. He should be thankful every day that you grace him with your presence. You should know that above all else, he has your best interest at hand. Your heart and mind should rest because you feel safe in his presence.

Kenisha and I connected immediately. We exchanged phone numbers, and from our first conversation, which lasted four hours, I knew I had found a valuable treasure. Kenisha was easy to talk to, and nothing was off-limits during our conversations. We laughed and joked about everything under the sun. I could not get enough of talking to her. I remember on one occasion, I called her after I got off work. We talked all night until the sun came up. We were amazed by the fact that we had talked all night. Neither one of us wanted the conversation to end, but I needed to sleep, and she had to go to work.

On our first date, we decided to go to the movies to see the new *X-Men* film. We lived in opposite directions of each other, so I thought that it was best if we met somewhere in between. We decided to meet at a strip mall near our church. When Kenisha arrived, she got in my car, and we proceeded to the movie. I could not keep my eyes off her. She was a true vision of loveliness. I was so excited to be with her, but I tried my best to play it cool. When we were walking into the theater, I did take note of her figure as she walked through the door. I looked up to God and smiled. God had answered my prayers because her body was perfect.

After the movie, I took her back to her car because she had to work the next morning. We both didn't want the night to end, so we sat there for a while, talking. Suddenly, a storm arose, and the rain was coming down so hard, you could not see past the windshield. I told her that she should wait until it stopped raining because I didn't want her to get wet. Kenisha looked at me with this coy smile and nodded in agreement. The rain did not stop coming down. It seemed like it would never end, but we were not concerned.

Time seemed to slow down, and I noticed Kenisha staring intently into my eyes. I wanted to kiss her, but I refrained because I wanted to respect her. I cared about her and wanted to do everything the right way. At one point in the conversation, she asked me why I kept looking away. I told her I was checking to see if the rain had slowed, but in reality, I was looking away to keep myself from leaning in to kiss her. My attraction to her was off the charts, and I knew I would fall if given the chance.

The rain finally ended. As I walked to her car, she turned to me and asked for a hug. I was so nervous, but I leaned in and gave her a friendly hug. She laughed a little and asked why I was so shy. I was speechless, but I told her that I wanted to be a gentleman. Kenisha was impressed by my answer, and I could tell that I scored major points with my response. She got in her car and waved goodbye. As she drove off, I could see her smiling, and I knew that we were going to be a couple soon.

During our dating, we had casually talked about marriage and what our expectations were for our prospective mates. Kenisha had great taste in almost everything, so I knew I had to step my game up with her engagement ring. I went to my jeweler to talk it over with him and to get an idea of what my budget needed to be. I wanted her to be blown away when she saw it. We looked at a lot of different stones, and I finally settled on the main one. Then we worked up the design for the ring and how I wanted the finished product to look.

I have nothing against the cookie-cutter jewelry stores at the mall, and they do serve a purpose. Many can't afford to go to a private jeweler. I just knew that Kenisha was special, and she deserved a special ring to commemorate my love. She was a rare precious jewel in my eyes, and I wanted to show my appreciation. She deserved the best because God had given me His best.

It took the jeweler about two weeks to finish the ring, which worked out perfectly because Valentine's Day was coming up. I wanted everything to be special. With this woman by my side, I was on top of the world, so I chose a restaurant that overlooked the city. I made reservations at Coach Insignia, which was located at the top of the Renaissance Center. It had spectacular views of Detroit and Canada at night. It would be the perfect place to ask her to marry me.

When the time came to pick her up for our date, I noticed that she was wearing a stunning outfit. I almost dropped to the ground and proposed right there because she looked so beautiful, and I couldn't take my eyes off her. I had selected some romantic music for our drive into the city. The whole time, I could barely concentrate on the road as so many thoughts raced through my mind. I did my best to play it cool, but my nerves were on edge the whole time. I was about to propose to the most beautiful woman on earth. In my mind, I wrestled with all of the details and how I was going to propose to her. I had to take several deep breaths to get my thoughts in order.

When we arrived at the restaurant, my nerves started to tingle and my breathing got a little heavy as we rode the elevator up to the restaurant. I am afraid of heights and don't like riding in glass elevators where I can see how high I am going. This added to my anxiety at the time, and even Kenisha noticed my uneasiness. She looked at me and laughed because I would not go near the glass. Then she looked into my eyes and reassured me that the elevator would not fall.

We had a wonderful dinner that was filled with delicious food and warm smiles. We talked about how we didn't really get into the huge emphasis placed on Valentine's Day. We both felt like every day should be Valentine's Day and that you shouldn't need it to show a person how special they were to each other. She said that as long as I bought her flowers through the year, I didn't have to pay triple the price on Valentine's Day. I agreed and told her that she would never have to worry about that with me.

Afterward, we sat and talked for a moment as we looked at the view through the window. Ahead of time, I had let the staff know that I was going to propose, so they gave me all the time that I needed. The server cleared the table, and she gave me that look and smile as if to tell me that it was time for the main event. Since our table was near the window, I asked her to get up and look out over the city. She was mesmerized by the view of the city. I could see the reflection of her smiling as she remarked at how beautiful the city looked.

At that point, I knelt behind her on one knee, and as she turned around, her eyes lit up like Christmas lights. She gasped and smiled as I professed my love for her. At that moment, time stood still as I asked her to marry me. I didn't notice that while I was proposing, the other tables around us stopped to take in the spectacle that was unfolding before them. With a voice that could summon angels from heaven, she looked at me and said, "Yes!"

The couples around us began to applaud as I rose to kiss her. We stood there in a warm embrace, looking into each other's eyes. The server and management came out to congratulate us. For a moment, you would have thought that we were the most popular couple in the restaurant. My proposal definitely stole the show.

This was the beginning of our journey toward oneness, and the fairy tale was being written right before our eyes. However, I did not know that this fairy tale would be short-lived. There was an enemy lurking in the shadows that would alter the course of our lives and change me forever. Fairy tales don't always have a happy ending.

ALPHA TO OMEGA

Our marriage was beautiful and special. My dreams, hopes, and prayers had come true with Kenisha by my side. Let me be clear: Marriage requires work. Nothing is ever perfect, but what I found in Kenisha that was lacking in my previous marriages was her willingness to make it work. We had our ups and downs in our first year, but we resolved to always let love conquer all.

The power of love is amazing, and it can perform miracles in the midst of disagreements and arguments. Kenisha never let go of that, and at times, she would run me up one side of the mountain and down the other. However, she would always come back to me because her love for me forced her to work it out. This made me love her even more, and I knew that our love was unstoppable. We were partners, friends, and lovers through thick and thin. She had my back, and I would do anything for her.

Kenisha's love was amazing and special because she taught me so many things and calmed my spirit whenever I felt anxious. She had this ability to touch and speak to my heart as if she was reaching into the deepest depths of my soul. We were truly connected in every way, both physically and spiritually. It was as if she was made just for me, like God had taken a piece of me and fashioned it into this amazing woman. Our future looked bright, and I knew that we would grow old together and raise many children.

Kenisha was a great mother to my daughter, and I looked forward to having children with her. I knew that our babies would be beautiful and blessed because she would raise them up to respect God. Every time we made love, I told her that I couldn't wait for her to get pregnant.

After so many months, we noticed that we were struggling with infertility issues, so Kenisha, being the trooper that she is, set out to identify what was blocking her conception. We went to doctors and specialists, seeking some opinions. She even looked on the Internet and began to change her diet, but nothing seemed to change. To all those that are out there dealing with infertility, my heart goes out to you because it is a trying time for a couple, although I believe that infertility is more difficult on women because your identity is wrapped around conception and bearing children. When a woman can't conceive, it makes her feel inadequate and less than herself.

Through it all, I remained confident and tried to keep her spirits up. We already had a name picked out for our baby, so as an act of faith, we put the names on the door that was to be the future nursery. Our girl was to be named Savannah Grace, and our boy would be named Ethan or Ian. We would pray in that room for hours, asking God to give us a child. Scriptures from the Bible were posted on the walls of the nursery, which we recited in faith every time we entered the room.

As the months went by, Kenisha would not be swayed. She continued being faithful and was full of hope. Months turned into years, but we kept on trying and praying. Being a man, I sought answers to our situation because all I wanted was to give her a child. There was a problem that needed to be fixed, and it was up to me to find the solution.

My first thought was she was having a problem conceiving due to the stress that she was under with her decision to go back to school. She had always wanted to be a registered nurse, and she had found an accelerated program that would give her a bachelor of science degree in nursing. This program was very rigorous, and she was unable to work because the course load was demanding.

When we had sat down to discuss her going back, I knew that it would be a struggle because I would have to handle all the bills on my own. At the time, I was working part-time for Delta Airlines as well as trying to run my own business selling insurance. My entrepreneurial pursuits had hit some snags and it was not going as I had planned. She wanted me to keep the job at Delta because she enjoyed the travel perks that I received. We could fly anywhere in the United States for free, and if we traveled overseas, all I had to pay were the taxes on the ticket.

I couldn't go back to corporate America because the work schedules conflicted with one another. The sales job was perfect because it allowed me to have flexibility with my schedule so I could keep working for Delta. I had no choice but to stick with developing my own business or finding another way to make money as an entrepreneur. However, she told me that as soon as she graduated, she had job offers lined up for nursing because her field was in demand. This meant our struggles would come to an end once she graduated. I was still a little hesitant in my mind, but I knew she wanted this chance more than anything. It was her dream to become a nurse, so I could not disappoint her.

We laid out a plan for the year, and we agreed to move forward. It was a tough year, and we had many ups and downs, but we stayed the course. There were times when I wanted her to throw in the towel because we were struggling with bills, and she was running out of money to pay for the program. However, God always made a way for us to keep our heads above water, and she managed to find scholarships and grants to pay for school. In my mind, I thought that maybe it was good that she didn't get pregnant because a child would have added more stress to our lives. I came to the conclusion that she would conceive once things calmed down. However, that did not stop us from trying. We kept the faith through the journey toward her graduation.

The time finally came, and Kenisha had reached her goal of becoming a registered nurse. We were both excited about her accomplishment. It had felt like we both went to school during this process, so my joy could hardly be contained as well. Her perseverance and determination to finish was admirable, especially since she had to overcome many obstacles along the way to achieve her goal. I think many would have given up and thrown in the towel, but her unwavering faith gave her what she needed to make it.

A sense of relief swept over us because Kenisha was going to work in the field that she had always dreamed about. Ever since I could remember, she had always told me of how much she wanted to be a nurse. Kenisha had to take a few detours along the way, but she never gave up. And as promised, she had a job before she graduated.

Kenisha received an offer from one of the hospitals in the area to work in their orthopedic unit. Although this was not the assignment she desired, Kenisha jumped at the chance and smiled every day that she had to go to work.

After about four months of working there, her dream job became available at another hospital. Kenisha had always wanted to work in labor and delivery because she loved working with babies.

She was a natural with children. No matter where we went, babies and kids were drawn to her. There were several children at our church that would look for her every Sunday. After service, they would come running up to give her a hug or tell her about something they did in school. When she held babies in her arms, they would look at her and smile with a look of wonder and joy. I was in awe of her gift with children and knew that Kenisha was going to make a terrific mother to our children.

When Beaumont Hospital called to offer her the position, her screams of joy sent shockwaves through the house. I remember her running upstairs to tell me the good news. The look on her face was full of excitement, like she had just won the lottery. Everything was working out, and we were well on our way to living the kind of life that we had dreamed about.

The journey to this point was very difficult and stressful, so we decided to reward ourselves with a vacation to get away and relax. Kenisha had wanted to go to Tahiti because she liked the pictures of the water. She had this fascination with the crystal clear blue colors that she noticed in all of the photos. After speaking with some friends, they suggested that we should visit Thailand. They told us that we could get the best value for our money on everything from hotels to food and shopping. When she heard shopping, her mind was made up and she began to research everything about Thailand.

We researched hotels, things to do, and where to eat. We were so excited about this trip because we had never been out of the country before. This was going to be a new experience for both of us, but we promised each other to make these types of trips every year. We were going to Thailand for ten days, and our itinerary included Bangkok, Koh Samui, and Phuket. Most people would book a guided tour to make sure they went to all the best places. We chose to go on our own adventure and make things up as we went along.

I really liked that she was open to travelling and exploring with me. I thought most women would have been scared to go to a faraway place without any guidance, but Kenisha was different because she was with me all the way. She was our personal travel agent that took care of all the details. She found the hotels and things to do when visiting each location. What I admired most about her was the fact that when she put her mind to doing something, you could consider it done. She was the help that I really needed.

As the day of our departure approached, we made sure that everything was in order. A few days before the trip, she had complained of having an upset stomach, but we didn't think much of it. However, on the night before we left, she told me that she couldn't use the bathroom and felt bloated. I told her that she probably needed to take a laxative, so I went to the store and bought some over the counter laxatives. She took them, and I noticed they didn't work for her, but she didn't complain. We were both excited as we continued to get ready to leave.

The next morning, we awoke with joy because it was time to head to the airport. We were both smiling from ear to ear while loading the car with our bags. When we pulled out of the driveway, we looked at each other and said, "I love you" at the same time. Kenisha was always very affectionate, and she loved to hear me tell her that I was in love with her. We both would say it to each other at least three to four times every day. I believe that this repetitive confession made our love for one another grow stronger. When we both said it before leaving, we knew that this was the beginning of something special in our lives.

When we got to the airport, we walked to our gate to meet our friends who we were traveling with. Sitting at the gate was a huge 747 jumbo jet that I had never flown on before. It looked massive with its four engines along the wings. I have always been amazed by airplanes and how they fly, so this was going to be a treat for me.

The flight was a total of eighteen hours to Thailand with a layover in Japan. When we arrived in Japan, we were in another time zone, which was actually a day ahead of back home due to the fact that we crossed the international date line. Japan would be twelve hours ahead of Detroit time, so it was best to try to sleep on the plane to avoid jetlag. This was not an issue because we were flying in business class, which was like having your own personal hotel room in the sky.

We each had a self-contained pod on the plane that converted to a bed. This made the long flight bearable and comfortable. Delta Airlines has a solid reputation of spoiling people in business class because they treat you like royalty. The food and drink selections were phenomenal, which added to our excitement. Upon boarding the aircraft, we were given a glass of champagne before takeoff. Kenisha and I toasted one another, and I began to sing the song "Glamorous Life" by Fergie. I was happy that I could provide my queen with this trip after all of her hard work. We were definitely on cloud nine, and this was going to be a great vacation.

When we arrived in Bangkok, we were in awe of the fact that we had flown across the Pacific Ocean to another country and time zone. We were blown away by the ornate designs that we saw at the airport and during our drive to our hotel. The city was large, congested, and a little chaotic, judging by how people drove. It put us in the mind of New York, but this was New York on steroids!

We set out to explore the city and see all the temples. Bangkok has many Buddhist shrines and temples all across the city. Some are very ornate, and you have to stand in line to enter them. Women have to be covered and cannot show too much skin. When we went to one of the temples, a man came up to my wife and told her that she was too sexy. He kept repeating, "Too sexy, too sexy," and he gave her a shawl to cover up. We both laughed as he handed her the shawl, but in my mind, I knew that she was the sexiest woman alive.

The people were very friendly, and we found getting around easy once you learned the transit system. There is so much to see and do in Bangkok. The temples are amazing, but they also have one of the largest flower markets in the world. Flowers are very important to them in their worship of Buddha. I asked Kenisha if she wanted to go, but her mind was on shopping at this point. We went to the MBK mall, which is a huge seven-story tall mall in the city. It is the place to go for bargain hunters; however, Bangkok does have the more traditional stores in other malls throughout the city. The shopping is great, and you can literally find anything you want or you can have it made for pennies on the dollar.

Our money goes a long way in Thailand. We brought an empty suitcase with us just to be able to pack and transport the things we bought. This was suggested to us by our friends who told us to visit Thailand for the shopping. We bought a lot of clothes because you can have them custom-made and tailored. Custom-made suits only cost me about two hundred dollars, and I could have monograms and custom stitching done at no additional price. Needless to say, Kenisha was in heaven.

We were only in Bangkok for a couple of days, and frankly, that was enough because the city never sleeps. It became a little overwhelming after a couple of days, so we were looking forward to relaxing. We headed back to the airport to catch a flight to our next destination, which was Koh Samui. It was a short forty-five-minute flight to get to this beautiful island paradise. We enjoyed the beaches and the laid-back atmosphere while staying there. They also have great shopping on the island, so we bought more things while there. The temperature was steamy and humid most days with the nights being real pleasant and good for sitting at one of the numerous beachside restaurants or bar. Sitting there under the stars with my love made the world seem so peaceful. This was what life was made of, and we looked forward to enjoying all that it had to offer.

We left Koh Samui after a few days and continued on to Phuket, which was another island. We had to catch another flight in order to get there. I noticed that Thailand is huge, and you really need a lot of time to see all of it. We only scratched the surface because we wanted to go to other parts, but we didn't have the time. However, we knew that we would return to this magical place to further explore its beauty.

Phuket was trendier than Koh Samui. You could tell that it was a tourist mecca, but it was still beautiful. The beach that we visited was really nice because the waves were manageable, and the water temperature was perfect. They had this quaint beach bar nearby that had great drinks and snacks. It was very relaxing, to say the least. It was really easy to get around the island with scooters that we rented for cheap. This was the best way to see the island and take in all of its beauty. Phuket and Koh Samui were perfect and just what we needed. If we could have stayed another week, we would have, but there always comes a time for all good things to end.

The day was nearing for our return to the States. It had been a fun-filled ten days with lots of pictures and memories of our first international adventure. We were set to fly back to Bangkok from Phuket where we would spend the night and catch our flight home the following day. Kenisha had started to slow down, and I figured that she was tired because we had been doing a lot of activities. I told her to take it easy, and that's when she told me that her stomach was hurting. You could look at her and tell that she was in pain. I asked her if she had been to the bathroom, but she said that she had been unable to go for a few days.

In my mind, I thought that she was having a reaction to all the crazy food that we were eating. I figured that she needed a laxative and everything would be all right. However, it would be tough for her to take it seeing that we had a long day of flying ahead of us. I don't think that she wanted to be in the air and having to go to the bathroom, but I told her that we could get something before we left for the airport. She told me that she would be all right and that she wanted to wait until we got stateside.

To make matters worse, we had to take a different route because the flight that we wanted was oversold. Instead of going back through Japan, we had to fly from Bangkok to Los Angeles. On the flight, I could tell that she was in a lot of pain, and I tried to keep her comfortable as much as I could. I held her for most of the way and kissed her every so often to keep her calm.

When we arrived in Los Angeles, we had a layover of about three hours. This seemed like an eternity to wait because I could tell that she was getting worse as the time went by. I went to buy her a laxative and told her to take it. I didn't care where she had to go at that point. I just wanted her to feel some relief.

We finally got home later that night, and I took her home to lay in our bed. She was tired and out of it, so I told her to go upstairs, and I would get the bags from the car. Afterward, I went up to lay with her, and all I could do was hold her and tell her that she was going to be fine.

The next day, I told her that we needed to see a doctor, but there was a problem because our health insurance was not active yet. She had to wait for the next enrollment period, which was coming up in another month. I was enrolled under her insurance previously because Delta doesn't offer insurance to ready reserve employees. I didn't want her to suffer in pain, so I told her that we would just have to pay the bill. However, she managed to get a referral to a doctor that would see her without insurance. A friend of hers had told her about this doctor and how much he cared for his patients. He was reasonable and was willing to work with us on the payment.

So we scheduled the appointment and went to see him. When he took one look at my wife, he noticed that she was bloated. She looked like she was pregnant, and I even joked with her that she was keeping a secret from me. The doctor said that he needed to schedule some tests, but he knew that our insurance was not active. He wanted us to wait for the insurance because the test was very expensive. We really didn't have much choice because we had tried going to emergency a few times, and they denied treatment for lack of insurance. So my wife was forced to suffer a couple of weeks until the insurance kicked in, which really irritated me because I was unable to help her in her time of need.

Waiting seemed like it took forever, but the day finally came, and her insurance was active. The doctor had already scheduled the tests, so I took her to the hospital to prepare for the procedure. After all the waiting, she was in a lot of pain. I knew something was seriously wrong and prayed that they would find the problem and get her back to good health. On the way to the hospital, we prayed, and as she prepared for the tests, I gave her a big kiss and told her that I loved her. The doctor told me not to worry and that the tests would only take an hour.

I waited patiently in the waiting room as thoughts ran through my mind. I figured that they would find something simple which would require surgery, but once that was taken care of, she would be okay. When the doctor came out, he took me back to the room where she was and showed me the pictures from the test. I immediately knew that it was not a simple matter. I had sat in on some colonoscopy procedures back when I was a sales representative for a major medical supply company. I knew a little about the colon and what a healthy one looked like, but I knew that this was not the case with my wife. I don't know if my mind was able to process what I was seeing, and for a moment, I tuned everything out in the room.

As he looked at me, I could sense the hesitance in his voice as he looked me straight in the eye. At that point, the only thing I heard was him saying that he needed to admit her immediately. A large tumor was growing in my wife's colon, and it looked very bad. I was not an expert, but I could clearly see that the pictures of her colon looked bad. It is not what we expected nor hoped for. We were supposed to hear good news and not the bad news of a large tumor that was growing inside my wife.

I stopped for a moment to pinch myself to make sure that I was not in some nightmare. I desperately wanted to wake up and see that I had been dreaming. However, this was no dream, but I felt like I was being sucked down into a black hole as fear tried to grab ahold of me. I looked at my wife and gave her a hug. I knew that I had to be strong for both of us. I didn't want her to think that her man was afraid, so I told her that this was going to all work out. We were now on a journey into the unknown, and at that moment, so many thoughts raced through my mind as we sat in the room that would become her home away from home for the next couple of weeks.

We were waiting on the oncologist to come and talk to us, which seemed to take forever as time slowed to a snail's pace. During our wait, they took her to run more tests to see the extent of the tumor. When she returned, I gave her so many hugs and kisses because I wanted her to know how much I loved her. I really couldn't tell what was going through her mind at the time, but she did manage to smile and reassure me that she was going to be okay.

I remember sitting there, holding onto her hand for dear life during our moment of prayer. We both asked God to step into this situation and bring healing to her. We knew that God was the only one who could rectify this situation, so we stood on our faith as we waited and waited for the doctors to come with their report. I remember walking out into the hallway a couple of times to see if I could see them coming, but the only ones that came were the nurses that were assigned to her.

Finally, the door opened, and in walked the oncologist that had reviewed her test results. He greeted us with a smile and gave us his credentials. He was warm and inviting, which is something that we needed because we were in a state of confusion over the fact that my wife had a large tumor growing inside of her that didn't present any symptoms nor warnings prior to a few weeks ago. The doctor began to go over the results as he pulled up her images on a computer that was in the room. He showed us the CAT scan results, and it presented a troubling picture to both of us. She had not one tumor but several that were growing in her body. There were tumors in her liver, her lower spine, and across the wall of her stomach.

I tried to keep myself from showing the utter horror that I was feeling because I wanted to be strong for my wife, but the images made me cringe inside. We both remained calm, and I was surprised that my wife took the news without crying or getting emotional. Maybe we were both in shock and there was a delayed reaction that was yet to come, but we remained silent as the doctor went over more test results. It was at that time that my brain began to come out of the initial shock, and I noticed that the doctor was talking to us, but I felt in my spirit that he wasn't telling us everything that he knew.

I tabled the thought and asked him what type of treatment protocol was planned for my wife. I had so many questions, like what type of chemotherapy drugs did they plan on using, and would she need radiation therapy?

He answered everything and said that he wanted to get her started as quickly as possible. They would use chemotherapies to battle the disease because radiation did not have much effect on this type of cancer. He also said that he wanted to get the pathology report back so that he could see where the cancer started. It was important to know where the main tumor was located as this would help them determine where to focus their treatment regimens.

Once he was done, he asked us if we had any more questions. I told him that I wanted to speak to him outside to which he agreed. Before he left the room, he assured my wife that he was going to do everything he could to eradicate her cancer. The pathology report was crucial; however, he wanted more tests run to get a complete picture. We were told that she would be released in a couple of days once they had everything that was needed. When I heard this, I wish I could say that I felt a little less fearful, but there was still something that was troubling my mind.

When we walked out of the room, we stopped in the hallway, and as I looked at him, I tried to search for the right words to say. However, the only thing that I could ask of him is that he give me the straight answer. I told him that I could sense that he wasn't telling us every-thing and that I needed to know the truth. He looked at me with a look of despair and told me that he was sorry. I noticed that as he said it, he dropped his head and began looking back and forth.

I asked him why he was sorry, and it was at that point he looked me in my eyes and said it again. It was as if he was searching for the right things to say, but he finally came out and told me that my wife's cancer was very extensive. But his next sentence hit me like a punch in the jaw from Mike Tyson. As I write this, I can still remember the pain that I felt from hearing this man tell me that my wife only had eleven to twelve months to live.

I have never experienced pain of this magnitude. It was as if he had reached inside of me and ripped out every vital organ as I stood there before him. I wanted to scream and cry, but I somehow managed to keep it together. My mind was racing, like a horse in the Kentucky Derby, with questions of how this happened and what just happened.

I wanted to scream, "God, please wake me up from this nightmare!" But all I could do was look him in the eyes and tell him that we were people of faith.

It was all I could say because at that point, it was the only thing that I could cling to in the midst of this onslaught. I had to stand and present a strong defense. I knew that if I stood up for God, he would stand up for me. The army of fear was coming against me, but my God was able to slaughter the army without any hesitation. Above all, I knew that God had my back.

The doctor just stood there, saying nothing. I knew that he was doing his job and that he had to present the facts to me. Faith and God was not his concern. He was a doctor who relied on his medical education and what his years of schooling had taught him. Maybe he wanted to believe God with me, but his professional acumen had to remain in the forefront. I thanked him and turned to retreat to the room where my wife was waiting.

As I entered and looked upon her face, I could no longer hold it in as I walked toward the bed. The tears and all the emotions came gushing out of me with the force of a tidal wave as I slunk down next to her. She looked at me with this bewildered gaze as she asked me what was wrong. I looked her in the eyes and began to hug her with all my being as I searched for the right words to say. I really wanted to run and hide, rather than telling her of what the doctor just spoke. I struggled in those brief moments on whether I should say anything, but she kept on pressing me for answers.

It was at that moment that I looked her in the eyes and mustered the strength to speak. My voice trembled as I muttered the words of the doctor. I told her of his prognosis and how he had said that she only had a year to live. I was prepared for her to break down and fall into my arms; but on the contrary, she pushed me away and began to tell me to get my act together. She vehemently told me that she was not going to die and that she was confident that God would heal her. It was as if she got mad at the disease and was taking it out on me.

I was a little confused by her reaction to the news. However, I soon joined her in presenting a united front against the enemy that was seeking to destroy our lives.

A few moments later, a nurse came in to give my wife some pain meds and take some blood samples. The nursing staff was wonderful, and once they found out that my wife was a nurse, they really took her care on another level. I could tell that nurses stuck together, and they formed a sisterhood that was designed to make sure that they took care of one another.

Once the pain meds had kicked in, my wife fell asleep. There, in the solitude of that hospital room, I began to recount our journey to this place. I asked God how this could happen and why He let it happen to her. A few weeks ago, we were sitting in a beautiful hotel in Thailand, talking about our wonderful future; and now we were sitting here in a cold empty hospital room, praying for her survival. Was this a part of Gods plan? Would God bring us through this test of our faith and allow us to give Him the glory for saving her?

So many scenarios went through my mind as I struggled to make sense of what we were facing, but as the sun began to fade in the distance, I heard nothing from God. My fear was clearly speaking, and it was telling me that the worst was yet to come. I gave out a sigh and tried to close my eyes for a moment. I had been awake for the past two days without much sleep; however, sleep was nowhere to be found. All I could do was sit there and gaze upon my wife as she lay in that bed. My thoughts were centered on her and saving her life.

She was my queen, and as her king, I was sworn to protect her from all enemies. My land and my realm were under attack, and I was not going to allow this enemy to come in and destroy my kingdom. I had no time for sleep because I needed to prepare for the battle that was before me. I had to muster my most trusted guards to ready themselves for battle. I summoned every ounce of strength and courage as I settled in to watch over her. If cancer wanted her, then it was going to have to come through me to get to her.

Principles of Faith

The battle of our faith was at stake, and we went into this fight, standing on the Bible and all that it had to say. There was nothing that could get us to believe anything else because we had become so regimented in the principles of faith. Scriptures swirled through my head daily as I repeated them out loud.

Our bishop had taught us the principles of living a faith-filled life where we relied on God and His word more than the words of men. He taught us things to help us remember what we were supposed to do when faced with a test or trial. They were the ABCs of faith, which stood for ask, believe, and confess. We knew that we had to ask God for what we wanted Him to do and believe that He would do what was essential to seeing the results. You had to believe in spite of what it looked or sounded like.

We had heard the report of the doctors, but it was our job to seek God and ask for His divine intervention. Yes, your natural mind will try to go against you, but this is where your confession is the key to gaining victory. The word of God is powerful, and it can change situations that seemed hopeless. We were taught to confess the scriptures over our situations so that God would hear and react. This required constant prayer and study of the Bible.

When Kenisha was too tired or in pain, I would take up the slack and speak over her what we were believing God would do for her. We were literally standing on the mountain, proclaiming victory over every enemy that came against us. We wanted to saturate the atmosphere in the hospital room with every ounce of faith that we had. We played audible scriptures on our phones night and day. A friend from our church brought a CD player to the hospital along with numerous recordings of people confessing healing scriptures from the Bible. We always kept it going in the background as a reminder of the wonderful works of God. We were battling with every weapon that was at our disposal so that nothing negative could get to our faith.

This was the environment that we were used to since we had been attending Detroit World Outreach. DWO was known for standing on faith and all that it could accomplish. There were verified and documented miracles of how God showed up on behalf of the men and women of DWO. We were known throughout church circles as DWO-ites, and like a finely tuned army, we were taught to battle.

Our bishop, Benjamin Gibert, had stared death in the face and won the victory back in 2005 when he survived a virus that should have killed him or at least left him unable to preach or teach for the rest of his life. Everyone knew of his testimony, and he never hesitated to tell how God had brought him back. The doctors were confounded because they said that he would never preach again. However, God had another plan to show His glory.

Bishop's recovery was nothing short of a miracle. He confounded the doctors and all the naysayers. And this miracle produced a boldness in our bishop that was undeniable. We nicknamed him the Spiritual Hulk because he was a strong and mighty warrior who looked death in the eye and won! He was a mighty man of valor, and all of those that followed him gained strength and fortitude from him.

My wife and I served as armor-bearers to him and his wife. Armor-bearers in the Bible were charged with carrying the armor and weapons of the warriors that they served. It was quite an honor in those days to be in the service of a mighty warrior, so me and my wife held our positions with great humility and honor. We assisted them in preparing for services at the church and prayed over them before we would go into the sanctuary.

Today, the weapon of choice for a pastor is the Bible, so we would carry their Bibles and any notes or other things that they needed for their message. We also ran errands and delivered messages to other ministries within the church. To be an armor-bearer was a calling to serve, and through that service, you also gained insight on how to become a true leader.

This position gave us access to a lot of prominent pastors and teachers because our bishop was always being called to teach somewhere. We had to be flexible with our schedules because we were usually required to travel with them. In some respects, we became extensions of their family because we were around them so much. It was a joy to serve, and this gave us a closeness that I didn't realize that we were going to need in the coming days.

When we received the news of her cancer, we immediately let them know because we wanted their prayers and counsel. Both Bishop and his wife stood by us and gave us the utmost care and attention. I know that Bishop really loved Kenisha and that he considered her as one of his daughters. He would spend hours at the hospital with us, which gave me a lot of strength because I was able to tap into his faith and align myself with his confession of the scriptures.

He would sit in the chair across from her bed like a wise teacher beginning his lesson. He instructed Kenisha to repeat his confession of healing that he was speaking over her. He prayed and quoted scriptures that gave us hope. We were so confident that we would be victorious that I saw us standing before the congregation, giving our testimony of how the doctors said death, but God spoke life.

In my mind, I saw the members of our church shouting and

praising God for the mighty works that he had performed in our lives. Kenisha was already rehearsing the testimony in her mind, and I could see that having Bishop near her renewed her will to fight. I too was thankful and smiling for the first time in many days because I just knew that it was going to work out in our favor despite what it looked like. The spirit of defeat was looming in the distance, and we did everything we could to keep it out of our presence.

You would think that would be enough and that we would need no other fortification against our enemy known as cancer; however, the enemy of fear is slick and cunning. It searches for any small crack in your armor and tests every wall you have built up. Once it finds a breach, it looks to get in and assert its power. Fear is relentless in its attack, and doubt is its companion. They are a lethal combination punch that is designed to knock you down or knock you out.

It starts out as a small thought in your mind that can blossom into a full-blown vision in a matter of minutes. The mind is very powerful, and once the seed is birthed, there is no stopping it from producing a whole forest of negativity and destructive thoughts. I thought for a moment of what I would do without her by my side, but I quickly dismissed it and continued with my faith regimen. Little did I know that fear was already in the camp and taking ground silently in the background of my mind. I found myself having more and more thoughts about losing the battle.

One night, as I sat there in the hospital room, watching over her, a thought came into my mind that paralyzed me and literally ran me out of the room. I went to the bathroom to run some water on my face, but the thought kept increasing in my mind. I decided to take a walk to clear my head. It was late at night, and the floor was quiet. There were only the faint sounds of conversations coming from the nursing station as I passed. I noticed one of the nurses and gave them a faint smile.

As I walked down the hall, I noticed that most of the room doors were closed, but occasionally, I would walk past an open room and notice the occupants. Some were caregivers like me. They had the faint look of exhaustion in their eyes as they watched over their loved ones. Some would look out to me as I passed by to offer a smile or a brief look of compassion. It was in those quiet moments where we were able to reflect and recharge.

I took the elevator down to the cafeteria, which was closed, but they had a room with vending machines that served cold drinks, snacks, and sandwiches. As I stood there, staring at the machines to see if anything looked good, I noticed that my mind had drifted off to some unknown place. My focus had been switched from thoughts of food to this blank space in my mind where time was irrelevant. During this moment, the attacking vision had ceased its advance and allowed me a moment of peace.

Afterward, I returned to the room; and as I entered, I stood by her bed and stared at her while she was sleeping. She looked so peaceful as I knelt to kiss her on her forehead. I took my post in the chair next to her bed where I was to stand guard over her through the night. Sleep began to whisper in my ear for a few brief moments.

Suddenly, the thought came rushing back in like a tidal wave crashing onto the beach. Only this time, the thought was vivid and distinct.

In this vision, I saw myself at our church, sitting in the Green Room with the other ministers. I was dressed in a dark suit and could see that the countenance of my face was sorrowful and withdrawn. Everyone around me was silent but attentive to me as if they were there to serve me and not Bishop. I saw myself wiping away tears as my head hung down, and I could feel the intense weight of sorrow as it invaded my spirit.

At some point in the vision, I saw myself being led to the sanctuary by those that surrounded me. In a flash, I was now sitting in the front row, looking at my wife lying in the casket. The choir was singing one of her favorite songs, and all I could do was just sit there and stare at the casket. It was so real to me that I could smell the many flowers that surrounded her on the altar.

As I sat there in shock and bewilderment, I noticed the throngs of people coming to view her body. As they looked over her, they turned to me and offered their condolences. Some embraced me with hugs and kissed me on the cheek. Most had the same look of shock on their faces as they filed by me. The vision was crystal clear in my mind, and I immediately knew that it was an attack on my faith.

So I began to wrestle with extricating myself from the grips of this demonic onslaught by praying like I'd never prayed before. I followed up my prayers with a voracious recital of scriptures for over an hour, but the vision persisted. It was relentless and unwavering in its attack, landing blow upon gut-wrenching blow. I sat there in that room, fighting my best fight, but I felt my emotions getting the best of me. The tears were streaming from my eyes as I tried my best to resist the fear and doubt that this attack was producing in my spirit. I cried so hard that I couldn't see anything past the tears that were gushing from my eyes, like torrents or rain.

My mind began to swirl out of control as I began to wonder if I was strong enough to continue the fight. I felt myself on the ropes of defeat, waiting for the enemy to land his final punch that would send me to the canvas. However, I summoned every ounce of strength and faith that I could muster and gave one last push. One last scripture and one last prayer was all that I had left in the tank.

The needle was dangerously slipping past empty, and I knew I would soon face the inevitable fact of running out of gas. Finally, the vision began to wane in the morning hours, and I could sense its retreat. I was completely exhausted from fighting all night long as the sun began to rise in the sky.

As I turned to gaze upon my wife sleeping, I noticed the sounds of life coming from outside the door. The hospital was alive again, and everything was buzzing. The shift change was taking place, and the new nurse had just entered the room to check her vitals. She smiled as she wrote her name on the board, and then she told us that she was going to get my wife's next round of meds.

As she left the room, I noticed that my wife was staring at me. She asked me if I had slept because I looked exhausted. I hesitantly told her that I was in and out of sleep the whole night. I decided not to tell her of my battle because I didn't want her to worry, so I quickly changed the subject and told her that I was going to the cafeteria to get some coffee.

The Bible says that we should pray without ceasing. I tried my best to keep up my prayer regimen, but over time, I know there were times where I began to grow weary. Were my prayers working? Were they really getting through to God? I have witnessed many prayer warriors speak on how they battled the enemy by praying fervent prayers of faith. Hearing them speak on their exploits caused me to wonder if I was as good or as prepared as they were. I began to doubt my own abilities, even though I had witnessed many victories on the altar after praying for others. But I kept getting the sinking feeling that my prayers were not working.

Maybe my thoughts were too scattered. After all, I had so much on my plate that I could hardly think straight. I knew that I was in shock and was constantly trying to pull myself together. We practically lived at the hospital for weeks at a time, but I was thankful that the staff looked out for us each time. They would always give us a private room, which was great because it made it easy to keep the atmosphere charged with faith and prayer. The room was large, and we could invite people in to sit and relax with her. However, I had to maintain strict security because we didn't want certain people coming to visit. We had family members and church members who were kept on the outside due to their lack of faith.

Kenisha was very well loved by many, and there were a lot of curious people snooping around, wanting to know what was going on. Some inquiries were genuine, but we chose to keep our battle private. The church was giving the members general updates and asking everyone to pray, so we felt that this was the best approach.

My prayers had to be focused on her healing, but I had to be mindful of other negative forces swirling around us. I had to pray constantly for peace during this battle because my wife didn't want certain people around. We had issues with her father and her siblings. The relationship with her sister, Marcenia, had always been strained since I can remember. Kenisha wanted nothing but the very best for Marcenia, but as much as she tried to help her, she realized that it was a lost cause. She tried to reach out to Marcenia on numerous occasions, but her sister would never engage her fully in the relationship.

It is my opinion that Kenisha's sister was jealous of all her successes in life. Like I said before, Kenisha was a focused and driven woman who would not let anything stop her. I think that her sister felt intimidated to some degree and chose not to be around.

I tried to get along with Marcenia myself, but she was a tough nut to crack. She always seemed so nervous around me and she couldn't hold a conversation. I tried to engage her to get to know her better, but over time, I gave up. In any case, their relationship was not where it should have been, and Kenisha and I talked often about ways to repair the damage. Of course, when she got sick, that all took a backseat.

Her brother, Little Stan, was more down to earth and very cerebral for his age. He needed guidance and some structure, so we had allowed him to live with us for a couple of years. We helped him through high school, and it was my goal to prepare him for college. However, I was unaware that he was harboring some deep-seated jealousies of his own. We were both surprised by Little Stan's behavior because he had seemed so mild-mannered, but he began to rebel shortly before her illness.

Kenisha really loved her brother more than anyone else. She would always tell me about how she had raised him from a baby. She would take care of him as if he was her son and not her brother, so his rebellion was a severe blow to her. In hindsight, I believe that his anger and rebellion were directed at me; however, I am at a loss because all I did was try to be a big brother to him. I wanted him to succeed in life and get a good education. So I tried my best to mentor him and talk to him about his future. I thought we had a good relationship, but in the end, I found out that I was wrong.

Now when it comes to her father, Kenneth, I don't have enough time nor paper to write about this guy. I could write a whole book on his shenanigans. In the seven years that we were married, I can count on one hand how many times we saw Kenneth and his wife. Kenisha did everything humanly possible to have a relationship with him, but he never truly embraced our marriage. She reached out many times by writing them letters and inviting them to church; however, they chose to distance themselves from us.

I would later come to find out that Kenneth hated me, and he was upset that Kenisha had married me. Kenneth thought that I was too old for his daughter; however, everyone else applauded our union and thought that we were perfect for one another. I had always known of his hatred because on the day of our wedding, he cornered me in the bathroom with words of intimidation. That was the last time that I spoke to him.

Over the years, he would infrequently call to speak with her, but he never wanted to speak with me. Being the man that I am, I held nothing in my heart and gladly reached out to him when we found out about her illness. It had been years since we had spoken, and Kenisha wanted me to call him to let him know of her condition. When he answered, I could sense his insolence, and due to my exhaustion, I was on the edge. I bit my tongue on several occasions when I spoke to him to give him updates. But on one fateful night, I could take no more of his venom and I lashed out in full anger. I asked him why he was being so nasty toward me when all I ever did was love his daughter.

He snapped back with a few choice words, and that's when I went at him with the fury of a heavyweight boxer. I think that I was letting go of seven years of disrespect and pain. The pain was the pain that my wife felt over not having her father in her life. Kenisha would lay in my arms and lament to me of how she had always wanted to be close to him, but every time she reached out, she was hurt by his lack of care. As her husband, I felt it was my duty to protect her, and at this point, I considered Kenneth a threat to our environment.

We allowed him to come to the hospital, but whenever my wife had enough, I had to escort him out. It got so bad that we eventually restricted his access to the room. I had to put a pass code at the front desk, and if you didn't know it, you were not allowed to come to the room. I would have never thought that her family would give me so many problems, but I am just giving you a glimpse into their distractions. There were so many instances of their neglect and lack of care, but I had to put it to the side and remain steadfast on my wife and her healing.

As you can see, I had to manage these mini battles at the same time while managing the main war. This caused a great strain on me because I wanted to let them know what was going on, but I had to be careful. I really could not rely on any of them to help me because I knew how they felt. However, despite their own personal feelings, I continued to try to extend the olive branch. I wanted them to spend time with their sister. Maybe they could have reconciled their differences or just put them aside and be there for her.

I really didn't care what they thought of me. I was not the one who was lying in the hospital bed suffering from a deadly disease. Their sister was battling a very aggressive form of cancer, and she needed all the love and support that she could get. Every time I reached out to them, I had to pray before I spoke because I really didn't want my anger to get in the way. This all proved to be futile because they chose to stay away. I invited them over to the house on several occasions, but in the six months of her illness, they only came once.

We found out that her brother was dating a girl that lived a mile from us. He could have come over many times, but I guess that he chose not to come because of his feelings toward me. However, he still could have come over, and if he didn't want me around, I would have left and given them their time. It was not about me, it was about Kenisha and what she needed. I was willing to do whatever it took to bring her peace and comfort. She had enough to deal with on her mind, and I wanted to limit her stress as much as possible.

I tried my best, but I can't be responsible for grown men and women. It is not my job to teach you how to behave in this situation. They should have known that they needed to squash all the petty differences and focus on helping their sister to heal.

I am thankful that not everyone in her family acted this way. Kenisha had an uncle and an aunt that she was very close to her. Uncle Nick and Aunt Gay stayed by our side throughout the battle. They were constants in our lives since the day we got married, and I really appreciated their love and support. They were the only ones that would come to the hospital and tell me to go home and rest for a couple hours while they sat and watched over Kenisha. I know that this was not easy, seeing that they had experienced this type of trauma before with the death of their sister, Carmeta, who was Kenisha's mother. But just like some seasoned vets, they came alongside of me and held both of us up.

Kenisha's grandmother Lucille had been in my corner from the first day that we met. Lucille knew how to handle Kenneth, and she became a buffer between me and him. She would often tell me to relax and let her handle Kenneth because she knew he was a handful.

All in all, these three warriors were all that I needed. They were truly a gift from God because their presence made the difficult manageable. I really don't know how I would have made it if it wasn't for them. I knew that they were praying, even when my prayers had ceased due to exhaustion or doubt. I was in a war, surrounded by my enemies, and all I had were a few allies in the distance.

The storm was raging all around me, thunderous booms roaring in my ears followed by waves of emotions that I was not prepared to handle. I was beaten and battered by the raging wind that was coming against me. There was no shelter that could withstand the onslaught that was seeking to destroy me. All I could do was cower down on my knees for protection.

It was as if I was being hit by a thousand hurricanes all at once. Wave after wave pounded against me, seeking to get me to give up and surrender. I cried out to God to save us as one who has lost all hope of survival. I wasn't really concerned about myself because I was not facing the monster that was attacking my wife. I really focused on the victory over the demon called cancer. It was truly an evil spirit that invaded our territory. I knew that calling it out by name gave me authority over its presence. That same authority gave me the right to cast it out, or so I thought at the time.

Yes, I was attacked on all points, and we both were in the battle for our lives. But I had to focus on her because her life was truly at stake. My prayers went up, and I know others were praying as well. The entire church was put on alert, and I knew that we had some strong warriors praying. I guess I really expected the glory of the Lord to come down and smite the enemy. Or I would have even settled for one of the many angels in heaven to come down and give us a good word of victory. However, there was nothing but silence across the land and in the heavens.

The silence spoke volumes as I began to face the fear and doubt of winning this battle. However, I began to pull scriptures from the deep recesses of my mind that justified the silence. I recalled the scripture where Michael was held up by a messenger of Satan in delivering the answer to Daniel's prayer. I figured that this must be the case because Kenisha was so special and powerful. I pictured God sitting on the throne, dispatching His angels to do battle against the evil forces. Like swift hawks, they flew from glory, down through the heavens, battling every foul spirit in their way. There was nothing that could stop them, and even when the enemy sent his best demons to block them, they eventually prevailed.

So I prayed harder and confessed every scripture that came to my mind. I searched the Word of God for any and every weapon at my disposal. I even prayed for those angels that were on the way. In the midst of this stand, I still heard nothing. This was so unusual to me because whenever I had asked God for anything in the past, I always heard His voice.

I know what it's like to hear from God. There have been many instances where I prayed and received an answer. They didn't always come right away, but it never took over a week or two to get a response. God would always let me know by giving me a scripture or sending someone to confirm His approval or disapproval of my request. So what was the holdup? I'm not used to silence, and it was quite unsettling. I needed to hear from Him on how He was going to give us the victory.

My mind was fixated on hearing from Him. So much so that I held on to every word that my Bishop spoke. He said that she was going to get through the battle, but it was going to be tough. This gave me hope, and I thought that God was speaking through him to give me the answers that I was seeking, but it still bothered me that I was not hearing anything. The attacks were loud and clear without a doubt. The thunderous roar of defeat remained in the atmosphere as I struggled to drown them out. The visions of her funeral continued to fill my mind with fear and doubt. I really needed to hear the voice of God, but once again, there was nothing but silence.

I was all alone and left to fend for myself. The enemy of my soul was accusing me day and night. His voice was resonating in my ears, but the voice of my Savior was nowhere to be found. *Did you abandon me, God? Did my sins totally separate me from Your presence?* I asked for forgiveness and repented from all that I had done or thought, but there was no atonement, and the silence remained.

In the silence, the attacks grew stronger while I grew weaker. The enemy was really having his way with me as he mocked me and ridiculed my faith. I could hear him saying that God had abandoned me and left me to my defeat. "Where is your God? He won't save her, and He won't speak to you. Give up and let go. Why continue to believe that He loves both of you? He doesn't care whether she lives or dies."

I fought back with all that I had left in me, hoping that a miracle would come to save my beloved wife. I believed right up until the end that God would turn it all around. I thought that He was testing our faith to see if we would really give up. I didn't want to let God down, so I continued to hang on and believe that it would all work out in our favor. We would show Him that we were serious about our walk with Him and that surrender was not in our vocabulary.

I recited Hebrews 11:1 over and over. "Now faith is the substance of things hoped for, the evidence of things not seen" (NKJV).

I was a mighty man of valor with my sword and shield ready for battle. I had been trained for this over the years, and now I was on the battlefield, fighting against an enemy that I could not see. I knew that I had an army of saints and angels fighting on my behalf, but I felt like I was all alone. I refused to believe that God had abandoned me. He was just off in the background, waiting to swoop in at the last moment. So I accepted the fight and took on the Goliath of my faith.

As I stood there in the wake of the battle, I saw nothing but desolation all around me. In my mind, I knew I was losing; however, I continued to stand strong and not think of impending defeat. I cried out for God just like Jesus cried out for Him on the cross. "My God, my God, why have you forsaken me?" (Matt. 27:46 ESV).

In the distance, I could see the darkness approaching as it slowly drowned out the light. I began to feel God turning His back on me just like He did when the sin was poured out on Jesus while He hung on the cross. That was the most intense feeling of loss and abandonment that I had ever felt. My heart ceased to beat in my chest, and the cold icy grip of fear took ahold of me. I saw my beloved Kenisha slipping from my grasp, and I was forced to let go. There was nothing I could do to save her. I failed, and my fight was in vain.

There was silence in heaven as darkness and all the evil forces hovered over me. I sank to my knees and bowed my head down in preparation for the final blow. The taste of defeat rose up in mouth like putrid sewer water while the smell of death left its stench in my nostrils as I gasped to catch my breath. I could not move and I could not think. All I heard was the laughter of the enemy as he shoved the defeat down my throat.

As I stared into the eyes of death, I resolved within my spirit to give up. As any beaten warrior not wanting to die slow, I hastened the forces to finish me so that I could die with honor. My love, my life, and my friend was gone. Death would not come for me as I was left alone and defenseless in the darkness of battle. The cruel gift of the enemy was to leave me beaten and battered. Death for me would have been easier to handle, but he forced me to witness the death of my true love, Kenisha V. Lomax.

As I stood there over her bed, looking at her lifeless body, my mind went blank. In six short months, cancer had taken the life of the greatest gift that God had ever given me. In the background, I could hear the screams and moans of those that loved her weeping in anguish. I searched her body for some sign of life, but she lay there, still and motionless. I sank to my knees by her side and laid my head on her chest. I didn't want to let her go, and maybe in my mind, I was attempting to call her back to me. Maybe God would hear my prayer and grant me one last reprieve. However, there was nothing but silence in her body, and as I raised my head to look into her lifeless eyes, a deep and powerful scream from the pit of my stomach rose up and filled the room. The tears were streaming from my eyes, and I could no longer control myself.

For six months, I had tried to be the great pillar of strength and the mighty man of faith! Now my kingdom was toppled and my borders were breached. My beloved queen was gone! What was I going to do now? How was I going to cope? And how do I go on without my queen by my side? I was lost in a great sea of shock and disbelief as my mind struggled to process the information. As a man, I was trained to overcome adversity at all costs. I was fashioned for battle, and defeat was not an option. In that moment, I questioned everything about my beliefs and my faith in God. Was it me who failed? Or was it God who failed me? My mind was awash in question after question until it could no longer process information.

In an attempt to protect itself, I could feel my mind shutting down. The screen went blank as if some force hit the reboot button in my brain. When I came to, I was still by her side, and my friend was behind me, telling me we must call the funeral home to pick up her body. I will never forget that image of her lying there. It is seared into my brain forever and ever. Death had won, and I was truly broken. Man down! Man down! Lomax has been hit! Lomax has been hit!

Time to Say Goodbye

After leaving the hospital that night, I came home to an empty and silent house. My mind was racing with thoughts of her lifeless body lying there while the undertaker prepared to take her away. I remember my friend taking me out of the room and telling me to leave because I didn't need to see them rolling her body out in the bag. Everyone asked me if I was going to be all right going home, and some offered to come with me, but I declined because I just wanted to be alone.

It was the dead of winter, and the snow was falling as I looked out of the window in the living room. I guess I was standing there, hoping that she would pull up in the driveway and honk her horn like she always did when she wanted me to wait up for her. I walked all around the house, staring at her medications and the medical equipment that was supposed to keep her alive. My mind had ceased to process reality, and I was living in this altered state of consciousness.

As I went upstairs, I looked down the hallway at our bedroom, and for a moment, I was scared to go in. I don't know why fear had taken ahold of me, but I felt so uneasy as I slipped into bed. The bed was cold and empty. I reached over to the side where she slept and grabbed her pillow. I breathed in deeply, trying to catch a faint smell of her presence or something to remind me of how she used to feel sleeping next to me.

I drifted in and out of sleep, but I had nightmares the entire night. I dreamt that I was standing in front of her closet and the door was closed. I could hear screaming on the other side, and I noticed that there was a light on inside that I could see coming from under the door. In the dream, I remember feeling scared to look under the door because I knew it was a nightmare. However, I summoned the courage to peek under the door, expecting to see some gruesome figure that was making the noises. As I looked, I saw nothing but light. There was nothing scary at all under that door, but I continued to hear the screams.

I woke up and wondered what the dream was about, but I couldn't come up with any explanation. Why did I hear screams? And what did it mean? Was she really at peace in her transition? Or was she somewhere that was scary and cold? I tried to come up with some answers, but my mind and my body were drained, and I couldn't process the thoughts. I just lay there, wondering if it was all just one continuous nightmare. I was really hoping that I would wake up and see her face looking at me with that bright beautiful smile. However, that was not the case because reality soon kicked in when the phone rang.

It was the funeral home calling to confirm my appointment to go over the arrangements. Three days earlier, we were celebrating her thirty-second birthday, and now I had the arduous task of planning her home-going celebration.

When a loved one dies, the person that is left to handle the arrangements has a tremendous task on their hands. There are so many details that need to be worked out, and you must enlist the help of others. Being in the military taught me to focus on tasks without distractions, so I guess instinct kicked in because I really didn't think about her in that moment. It seemed kind of strange to me that I wasn't a complete mess. I felt sad, but I guess the shock of everything dulled the pain for the moment. Anyway, I had to go to the funeral home to talk about the arrangements.

I am so thankful that her Aunt Gay and Uncle Nick came with

me. They tried to stay out of the way and give me full respect, but I wanted them to be with me in the process. They were the only ones along with Grandma Lucille from her family that were there for both of us from the start. Their presence at that moment helped me to feel at ease. As we sat there, going over the paperwork, I was trying my best to stay focused. I had never done this and really didn't know what it took to plan a funeral. We finally got done, and then the funeral director gave me another list.

I had to pick out her clothes and accessories, go to the florist, and meet with the printing company to get the obituary done. I delegated the task of picking her clothes to a couple of her friends from the church. They came over and looked through her closet to find the perfect suit. They put everything in a bag for me to take to the funeral home. Then we sat down to talk about the obituary. I love to write, but this task was too much for me. I once again went into delegation mode and asked her play-sister, Tere McKinney, to write the obituary. I gave her a rough outline to follow, and Tere took it from there.

Tere did a phenomenal job. She really told Kenisha's story in such a way that highlighted all her accomplishments and accolades. Like I said before, I really am thankful for the team that assembled around me to make all of it happen. Her friends stepped up and stood by me the whole time. They were not even related to us, but they helped me with everything. I wish that I could have had Marcenia and Little Stan there with me, but they were not involved in the process.

The day had finally come for the public viewing at the funeral home. I and close family would be the first to see her before others arrived. As I walked into the chapel, I could feel my heart beating and racing in my chest. I really was not prepared for the moment, but I took a deep breath and walked up to the casket. Kenisha looked so beautiful lying there. Kenisha was just sleeping, and soon she would wake up and smile at me. My beautiful wife was lying before me, and all I could do was stare at her in complete amazement. It was like seeing her for the first time all over again.

The tears began to stream down my cheeks as other family members embraced me. I was a mess inside, but I knew I had to hold it together. Others began to arrive, and so many people came that we had to move to a larger chapel. I was truly amazed at all the friends and family that showed up. Her coworkers and her professors from the nursing school came to offer their condolences. Everyone talked about how Kenisha was such a good person and how tragic this loss was. Coworkers from my job came to offer support. I was overwhelmed because I didn't think that many of them cared enough to come, but they really showed me love.

This outpouring helped me to keep my mind off the sadness and pain that I was feeling on the inside. I was so preoccupied with everyone that I really didn't think about crying. I went up to the casket several times to check on her and to gaze at her beautiful face. On one occasion, I noticed that Marcenia and Little Stan had arrived along with some other family members. I thought that we would have a moment to talk and offer each other support, but that was not the case. They all came in and walked right past me without saying a word. They sat over in a corner of the chapel and stayed to themselves.

Everyone asked me about them because they all noticed their behavior toward me. I shrugged it off because I didn't want it to ruin the evening. However, I did make a mental note in my mind and knew that they would probably try to disrupt things at the funeral the next day. Yes, it was sad how they chose to act. They couldn't put their animosity down for one day and come together with me to celebrate their sister whom they say they loved. So I just let them be and ignored the foolishness.

I went back to talking with all the guests who came to support me. I could have stayed there all night, and a part of me did not want to leave her. My friend had to force me to go home and rest because the home-going service was the next day. There was still a lot of people in the chapel when I left, but they understood that I needed to rest.

I left that night and made the drive home in silence. I didn't turn the radio on because I was lost in my thoughts. All I could see was my beloved wife in that casket. *Wake up, baby. Wake up. You've been asleep too long, and I want to talk to you.* My mind kept rehearsing it repeatedly, but I knew that I was dreaming. To this day, I don't know how I made it home because I can't remember the drive. One moment, I was thinking about her, and the next moment, I'm pulling up in the driveway. I drove over twenty miles, and it was all a blur.

On December 23, 2016, I laid my beautiful wife Kenisha V. Lomax to rest. Instead of planning for a beautiful Christmas, I was sitting in our church, preparing to say goodbye. The vision that haunted me months earlier in the hospital had finally come to fruition. I really didn't know if a lot of people would show up because I knew that they had plans for Christmas. I had thought about waiting until after the holiday to have the celebration, but it would have been too long of a wait. However, I was surprised at the amount of people that showed up.

The church was packed. As I looked over the seats, I thought to myself that she would be amazed at the outpouring of love that everyone showed. Kenisha never realized her impact on people. She had such a great spirit of humility, and it resonated throughout her interactions with people that she met. Everyone that came up to me to offer their condolences told me about how Kenisha touched their lives. I got hugged so many times that it all became a blur in my mind. To this day, I still can't remember all the people that came up to me.

It was hard to say goodbye to Kenisha because she had been by my side constantly for over eight years. That moment of the last viewing will always live in my mind. All the family members had their moment to go to the casket and say their goodbyes. Marcenia, Little Stan, and Kenneth made their way to the casket. I let them all go up first as was standard protocol.

As I watched them, I wondered what they were saying and how they were feeling at the time. Were they sorry for not being there in her last days? Were they thinking about apologizing to me for how they treated me during this whole ordeal? I guess that was wishful thinking because they finished and went back to their seats. They didn't even come over to me and offer any type of sympathy or condolence. I really didn't think that they would be that petty, but I guess I was wrong. They always acted like a bunch of immature idiots, so why should this be any different?

Next, my family went to view her body, and they all said their final goodbyes and went back to their seats. Finally, it was my time to say goodbye. I remember the lady who was going to close the casket telling me to take my time. I stood there for a moment and collected my thoughts. I really could not believe that this was happening. My mind was racing with so many thoughts. I thought I was still trapped in a dream, and in my mind, I was trying to understand what was taking place. My mind was caught up in a battle of fiction versus reality, and I was struggling to hold it together. If there was ever a time that I could lose my mind, this was the time.

I have always feared being near dead bodies. I guess I watched too many horror movies as a child. I would always think that the person was going to wake up and scare the life out of me. But this time, I was not afraid. Kenisha looked so beautiful lying there, like Sleeping Beauty. Her face was so radiant and at peace.

I said my goodbyes and leaned in close to her and told her that I would always love her. Then, without thought or hesitation, I kissed her on the lips and caressed her hand. The tears were streaming down my face, and I didn't want to let go. If I could have jumped in that casket with her, I would have. She was my one and only true love, and not even the fear of death could keep me from her.

As they closed the casket, I gave out a deep wail of pain. It was finished, and I would see her beauty no more. All I had to remind me of our love were numerous pictures of our life together. I would not hear her laugh nor see her smile again. It all seemed so final, and in truth, it was. A book had been closed, and it could not be reopened. The story of our life together had come to an end, and this was not how it was supposed to happen. We got cheated out of life together. We had planned on having a family full of children, but that was not to be.

How was I going to cope without Kenisha by my side? How was I going to go on and live? What right did I have to live and be happy when the one that I loved more than my life itself was gone? I was numb as the choir sang her favorite songs. Not even the comforting words of Bishop Benjamin Gibert could soothe my soul. I was in anguish, and my mind did what it needed to do in order to protect me. It totally shut down. That's why I am glad that they videotaped the entire service. Later, I would go back and watch it so that I could remember the things I forgot.

Some people thought that it was strange that I wanted to watch it, but they didn't understand the fact that I needed to see what I had missed. I needed that closure because my mind was trying to make sense of everything that happened, and I needed the details.

Mind Games

As I stated before, I have never had to do anything like this in my life. I have never heard anyone talk about the aftermath of the funeral. Most men I know need details and a clear-cut plan. Most men are not equipped to handle the emotional barrage that comes against us. I believe that's why God made the woman. She is the protector of our emotions, and she is there to help us navigate these complicated waters. However, my guide was gone, and I was left to try to make it on my own.

Some people checked on me from time to time, but soon everyone went back to their own lives. I don't blame them because they had their own responsibilities to take care of, but I was still lost and confused in a raging river of grief. I really felt defenseless as my emotions ran rampant through my mind and spirit. I felt disconnected from everything and everyone. There was no fight left in me, nor could I exercise any type of reasoning to help me move on. My soul was caught in the white-water rapids of pain and guilt.

Swept through circling currents of endless sobbing and weeping, my eyes unleashed tears that were so heavy that I literally felt as if I was drowning in them. I began to blame myself for everything that had happened during the battle. Circling back through the catalog of my mind, I came up with numerous reasons why she died, and it all pointed to me. Maybe it was my punishment for some forgotten sin that I committed years prior to meeting my queen. After all, some of my indiscretions were legendary, and I wasn't always a choir boy. God was enacting His judgment upon me, and the price that had to be paid was stiff.

I had been told so many times before that sin has a cost, and it must be paid. But as my mind went down this path of shame, I wondered why my sins were paid with the life of my queen. Why didn't God just take my life instead? He could have easily ended my existence for the things that I had done, but He chose to take something close to me and leave me to suffer the pain.

These and other ludicrous thoughts filled every space of my mind both day and night. My thoughts were all that I had at that moment because God was nowhere to be found. His silence was my proof that He had given up on me and left me to fend for myself. My sins were too great, and God was done. The cup of iniquity was full, and it was time for a little payback. God knew where to hit me. This blow would surely bring me to my knees and make me understand who I was dealing with. This was God and, in my mind, I knew that I had displeased Him. He was well within His right to exact judgement, and I didn't blame Him for my punishment because He probably had good reason to pronounce me guilty.

Waves of guilt washed over me as I thought about the past and how I was so clueless about her health. I searched every inch of my mind to see if there was some hidden clue as to why this went undetected. The thoughts came in succession one right after the other as I stood on the shores of my mind. Wave after wave crashed against my body, seeking to force me from my stance. Why didn't I get her to another doctor sooner? Maybe if I had taken her somewhere else, she would not have died. Or maybe they could have come up with something else to prolong her life. Did I really do everything I could have done to save her life? Or was I limited by our insurance?

I wanted to take her to some of the top cancer clinics, but they all wanted enormous amounts of money to see her. One well-known cancer center that advertises on television about how much they want to help told me that they would see my wife if I put down a cash deposit of $250,000. Yes, you read that right. They asked me for that amount without blinking. When I told them that was ridiculous, the gentleman on the phone told me that they never assumed what a person did or did not have. I could have been rich, I could have had access to a life insurance policy, or I could have had money in my 401k.

I kind of understood his assertion because we were talking on the phone, and he didn't have any idea who I was; but the fact that I didn't have that amount to save her really hit home. After I got off the phone, I sat back and cursed myself for not having the money. I convinced myself that if I had stayed in corporate America, I would have had better health insurance and access to life insurance policies that I could have cashed in. I felt horrible because I couldn't give her the best care that she needed.

In the back of my mind, I was still reeling over the amount. Does anyone have that type of cash lying around? And if you did, are you really thinking about using it to pay medical bills? Then it dawned on me that he said it was just a deposit. I soon came to realize that this disease is a cash cow for the doctors and the pharmaceutical companies. I really don't think that they really care about saving people because cancer is an industry within itself, and it brings in a lot of money.

I also believe that they have a cure for cancer, but why should they cure a disease that is raking in billions of dollars every year? When I was in the military, I learned about a term that was used in planning battles. The men in charge of the war try to calculate the amount of men and women that will be killed going into a battle. It's called acceptable casualty loss and it is justified as the price for victory in a war.

I believe that cancer has its own acceptable casualty loss as well. However, I don't believe that they are seeking victory. I believe that they cure a few to keep everyone's hopes alive, but they allow a certain amount to fall through the cracks. It is a win-win strategy that benefits pharmaceutical companies and doctors. It also helps to ring in the donations to all the so-called cancer charities.

Through my research, I have found that many of these foundations donate less than 10 percent of their donations to actual research and finding a cure. The other 90 percent goes to the CEOs and other administrative costs. Therefore, I do not donate to nor participate in any of their campaigns. The money could be better utilized by helping people like me who need access to other doctors and forms of treatment. It would also be nice if families and caregivers had access to donated funds to help with all the cost of caring for your loved ones.

Caregiving for a cancer patient is a twenty-four-hour job, and I had to be there for everything. Trying to work a job and render care to a cancer patient was hectic and stressful. I am thankful that my job gave me the time off to care for her, but time off meant no money. After exhausting all my vacation time, I had no income coming in for weeks. The savings had dwindled down to nothing, but the daily cost of living was still there.

I really wish that I could have gone to one of the charities and said I needed help. I am thankful for the caring souls who stepped in to help us get access to Social Security benefits and other government programs. This helped me to ease my mind a little, but the rest was short-lived.

It was a struggle to not give in to the thoughts of failure. My mind was attacking me left and right over not having the money that we so desperately needed. I kept asking myself every single day if I was really doing enough to save her life. A friend told me to do a Go-FundMe campaign to solicit donations from friends and family. I was a little skeptical at first, and my wife really thought that it would not work. I remember writing the description and thinking that I would only set the campaign to reach a maximum goal of $5,000. Instantly, I heard a voice in my head saying to ask for more, but hesitance to do so loomed in my mind.

After talking with the friend who suggested the campaign, we decided to set it to $50,000. At the time, I also decided to post Facebook Live videos to help boost the campaign and keep friends posted on our progress. A lot of people wanted to know how she was doing because she had a lot of people out there praying and believing that God would heal her. The response was overwhelming due to the amount of love and support that we received from those videos. People were watching from all over the country, and their comments were inspiring.

In that moment, I could rest my mind and get a little bit of a recharge. Everyone wanted to know how they could help. When I released the GoFundMe page, it literally went viral, and although we didn't reach our original goal, we did get over $25,000 in donations to her cause. To this day, I wish that I could hug every person who donated. You just don't know how much you helped us.

My wife was let go from her job after a few months, and I was working for the airlines part-time while trying to sell insurance. My insurance income decreased due to me not being able to be out there selling, which was impossible due to the fact that I was the only caregiver to my wife. Besides, how can anyone focus on a job when they are faced with the daunting fight against cancer. The love and support from those donations allowed me to spend that time with her without worrying about paying bills.

The support also allowed me to buy alternative medications to try to help her. I bought cannabis oil, black seed oil, and anything else I could find that had success in killing the cancer cells. I would have given anything so that she could live, including my own life for hers. My thoughts were solely focused on her survival, and I considered my sacrifice as a part of my duty to her and our love.

Recalling a memory from my mind, one night while Kenisha was in the hospital, I began to pray and talk to God. In that prayer, I begged God to give me her cancer. *Take me, Lord, for I would gladly sacrifice my own life for her to be healed.* My fervent plea was for God to take it away from her and put it all on me. If a life was required, then I would give mine because she did not deserve this suffering. He was God, and I knew that He could do anything. My love for Kenisha was so great, and I could not bear to lose her. On my knees in that room, I beseeched the Lord to send His angels with word of His decision.

As I knelt in the silence of the room, all I could hear was the buzz of all the machines that were hooked up to my wife. There would be no answer, no angelic visitation. All I could do was sit there and watch her while my mind continued to attack me. Was I really doing enough to save her? The question still haunts me to this day.

The mind is quite amazing in its ability to recall events and emotions that happened in your life. It has been some time since her death, and I have tried to move forward as best I can. However, I am plagued by what I call ambush thoughts that seem to come out of nowhere. They are thoughts of painful memories that totally take over my mind at any given moment. Some of the memories are so vivid, it's as if I am right back in the moment. They come on while I'm driving or just going about daily life. I have also dubbed them storms because like an approaching thunderstorm, I begin to hear the rumble in my spirit.

They usually start as low and dull aches in the back of my mind, followed by a rush of emotions that totally incapacitate me for a moment. I have learned to keep tissue handy for the onslaught of tears. One day, while driving to work, suddenly I was back in the hospital room, hearing my wife saying that she didn't want to die. Kenisha was sitting up in the bed with this sad look on her face as she began to tell me that she didn't want to leave me or Tristan. Death was not an option at that point, so I tried to console her and give her strength.

I looked into her eyes with the most positive look of assurance that I could offer and told her that she was not going to die. I tried to embrace her as best I could, but the pain was too intense, so she pushed me away. Kenisha was in so much pain that I could hardly touch her, but she didn't complain much. Soon, she fell back to sleep, and I settled in to watch over her.

How did my mind remember that moment? And why was it coming back to me? We had never really talked about the possibility of death. We just wouldn't accept it because we were so focused on the victory. But that memory gave me insight into facts that she kept from me. I believe that she knew the end was near, but she didn't want to tell me because she cared about me too much to see me in pain. Maybe in her mind, she thought she was sparing me from the sadness and the pain. In looking back, I really wished that she would not have concealed it so much because maybe I would have done some things differently. Maybe I would have given her more kisses and affection, even though I kissed her every day. Maybe I would have told her how much I truly loved her, even though I said it every day. Maybe I could have figured out a way to say goodbye because I never got the chance.

The last time we spoke was when they were transferring Kenisha to hospice. As they wheeled her down to her room, I remember her telling me that she was in pain. As we walked through the corridor, all I could do was try to reassure her that she was going to be all right.

That's the last time I heard her voice because the moment that she entered her room in the hospice unit, she fell back into a deep sleep. In her last days, she would only speak when she needed her medication. She would look at me for a moment, and then she would drift off to sleep. It pains me to think about it, and I really wish that things could have been different.

People who have never been through losing a loved one will never understand the amount of pain that grief brings. I know that we had a lot of good memories, but even remembering those are painful because it brings about the thoughts of your loss. It's easy to say, "Remember the good times." However, what do you do when the remembrance of anything makes you cry oceans of tears? I know there will come a time when I will be able to smile when I remember her, but getting to that point seems like walking through a maze, trying to find your way out.

Most people really exacerbate the pain by trying to tell you things like it's time to move on or just try to think about the good times. But in my mind, there are no more good times. I'm here all alone and left wanting to hear her voice again. My mind brings back times when I would just look at her in complete awe and wonder because she was so beautiful. Her smile, her laugh, and the fact that she truly loved me with all her heart resonates through my mind like the cadence of a marching army. There's no escaping the cascading thoughts of Kenisha.

It's impossible to go to any of the old places that we used to frequent. Our favorite restaurants and the stores that she used to love to shop at are now off-limits for me, like a crime scene wrapped in yellow tape. Everything about this city reminds me of Kenisha, and I wonder if I can continue to live here. I really wish that I could relocate to someplace that would not remind me of our time together, but for now, that is not possible.

My mind wonders if I can ever be free to live again, love again, or breathe again. Will my mind stop with the relentless assault of making me feel like a total failure and loser? The thoughts reach down into the depths of my soul and brings up emotions that overwhelm every part of my being. So like a coward running from a fight, I retreat in defeat to a quiet place to weep and mourn. When my mind unleashed its fury upon me, I was annihilated by the force of full nuclear arsenal that rained down on my position. The symphony of destruction begins to play as my mind recalls a song from long ago.

The rock band the Police sang a song called "King of Pain." The chorus floods my mind:

I have stood here before inside the pouring rain,

With the world turning circles running around my brain,

I guess I'd always hoped that you'd end this reign,

But it's my destiny to be the King of Pain.

Suddenly, torrential memories unleash their attack one after another to beat me to a pulp. I had to watch her die! I was not man enough to stop death and I was unable to fix the situation! I cycle through the last six months, like chapters in a book. I had to sit there and watch her go from this bright energetic woman to a lifeless shell. Our life that we had looked so forward to was now in ruins before my feet.

When I met her, I felt like I had finally won! I had beaten the odds and erased my previous failures. It felt so good to win and finally be at peace. Yes, she was the one who turned all my bad days to good. Kenisha was the one who made me smile every day I woke up and looked into her eyes. Our love was strong, it was real, and it was the truth. But now my mind reminds me that there is no hope for me. Maybe I was living in a fantasy, believing that I could achieve happiness. No, my destiny was pain, and I was the king of this afflicted kingdom.

My mind had taken ahold of me as I sank deeper and deeper into its tortuous realms. Insanity beckoned on the horizon, telling me that I was done and there was no escape. My hopes and my dreams were destroyed right in front of me. There was no way out of this hell called grief. In my mind, I was ready to give in and let my emotions take me down. It was time to stop fighting it and accept the fact that I could never be truly happy. I was the pawn of forces outside of myself that reveled in my destruction. It felt as if God and Satan were having fun with me while playing their heavenly game.

To them, I was some useless pawn on their chessboard. Neither one of them cared about me, but it felt like they delighted in my suffering. It was like they were sitting there, plotting the next move of my failure. So I decided to get off the board and check out of the game. I figured that if I was on my own, I might as well play by my own rules. I'll walk my own path like a rogue warrior cast out of his clan.

This could have turned into a dangerous decision, but I was ready for the consequences. After what I had been through, it couldn't get any worse. In preparation of my departure, I resolved to forget about everything and just live—no cares, no thoughts, no worries. It's my life, and I tried it your way, and what did that get me? Nothing but a swift kick in the teeth.

All of my beliefs and everything that I had been taught over the years were now being challenged. Most of them were rejected as nothing more than pure fantasy. But I could never really get away from the fact that I still cared, even though I didn't want to. As much as I wanted to tell everyone to go to hell, I still found myself reaching out to help others. I resented the fact that I couldn't be selfish and mean when my mind wanted me to be. Yes, my mind was telling me that I was a loser, but a miniscule thought of me winning kept surfacing. A barely audible voice was whispering in the background to not give up. It reminded me of the good that Kenisha saw in me and it did not hesitate to let me know that she was watching me.

As I pondered this thought, I saw my beautiful wife standing before me, smiling. Kenisha stood there, telling me that I could make it and that she was with me. She was encouraging me from beyond, and I felt the warmth of her embrace. The peace and love of God flowed from her eyes, and I knew right then and there that I had to get up and live for her. Kenisha was counting on me. She left her legacy with me, and she was a winner.

In my mind, I had to conclude that she was really gone. It was tough, but I had to accept the fact that she was no longer physically by my side. I had to come to grips with the fact that the life that I thought we would have was now a distant memory. There would be no more anniversaries nor vow renewal ceremonies. The hopes of our beautiful children being born were now just vaporous thoughts dissipating in the wind.

My mind forced me to accept that I wasn't going to grow old with her. It would have been nice to have a family that we invited over to dinners or holiday events. However, there would be no sitting at the table, looking out over our children and thanking God for a wonderful family. No, instead I was left alone with the memories of what was supposed to be. This was a bitter pill to swallow indeed. But I was reminded by my thoughts of her that she would always be with me in my heart. It was not the same, and I would have preferred her here with me, but that would have been selfish of me.

Kenisha was in a lot of pain, and the cancer had robbed her of the life that she wanted. She was a vibrant lively stone who was always on the go. Her ambition and energy was boundless, and there were several times during our relationship that I had to tell her to slow down. There was no doubt in my mind that she could not see herself being in such a dependent state. It would have been too much for her to handle. Kenisha was better off being with God and totally free of any disease or affliction. Her mother and her grandfather were there with her, so I didn't have to worry about her being alone. Plus, I knew that one day I would see her again.

I could imagine looking into her beautiful eyes once again and the smile that it would bring to my face. We would be united for eternity with nothing to keep us apart. Aside from Jesus, she is the first person that I want to see when I get to go home.

I also had to accept the pain of the loss instead of trying to run from it. The pain was real, and it was intense, but accepting it took away its power over me. Instead of trying to suppress the tears, I embraced them and let them flow. Yes, I still cry when I think about her or I visit one of our favorite places. But the emotions don't incapacitate me anymore, and I feel free to express them however they wish to manifest.

When the ambush thoughts come and try to take me back to the fortress of guilt, I remind myself that I did everything I could with what I had at the time. Learning to live with the pain seemed foolish at the time, but in retrospect, I have come to understand that the pain was necessary. Pain and grief are the cost of true love. If Jesus had to endure the cross for us, why should our journeys be any different? Christ's love for us came at a great price, and so did my love for Kenisha.

The mind can be a great resource, but it can also be your worst enemy. For a man, it is the place where the battle is first waged and the central point of attack. The scripture states that whatever a man thinks, he is that thought. So we must shield our minds from all negative and doubt-filled thoughts. I believe that men are more debilitated by grief and loss because we calculate everything in our minds. The mind is the focal point of our existence. It is where we meet God and reason with Him about the pathways that He chooses for us.

When something doesn't go the way that we think that it should, we quickly retreat to our thoughts. We go over every detail and intricacy to see where we may have failed or what we could have done better. It's our nature to question everything and demand answers so that we can achieve success the next time around. However, in this case, I was not able to question why this happened to me because God was not answering. I was left to try to sort through things on my own, and in some respects, come to my own conclusions. This is extremely taxing, and it has only served to frustrate me because I want to have some sense of closure. It is as if my mind is unable to rest because I'm always trying to figure out how I got to this place.

This one truth has been the most difficult one to accept, and I have tried to just let it go. Why can't I just accept the fact that none of this was in my control? Who am I to think that I knew better than God? But in the stillness of my mind, I can't help but wonder if things could have been different. Maybe it's time to stop thinking and start asking God to help me to let it go.

RECONCILIATION

Throughout this journey, I have experienced intense emotions that have shaken me to my core. My beliefs and my faith have been severely challenged, and at times, I have wondered who I am becoming. I have asked the question many times in my mind over the years if I was still walking with God or if I was a rogue agent on my own, trying to figure life out.

At times, I have found myself identifying with Viggo Mortensen's character in *Lord of the Rings*. He was known as the ranger because he held no allegiance to anyone or anything. He merely fought evil when it presented itself. I am not the same person that I once was, and I have questioned my salvation and my calling on numerous occasions. I have been forced to reevaluate what I have been taught about God over the years. At times, I have wondered if this should be an indictment on God and His love toward me because my trust in Him had been shaken. My disappointment in God and how He handled things have challenged me at times. Quite frankly, I feel like He let me down.

Should I blame Him? Or should I blame the enemy of God? The anger that I feel has not helped me to understand my feelings on this matter. At times, I have found myself welling up with indignation toward anything related to God, like praying or reading His word. I really felt like running away from Him because I had given Him my complete allegiance, and in return, all I got was a stinging defeat. This was not the mighty God that I was taught about in various churches. God couldn't fail, He couldn't be beaten, and He certainly had all the power.

So what went wrong? How could I trust him again? I was ready to let go and wash my hands of this so-called victorious walk of the Christian. But there was this little spark in the dark recesses of my spirit that kept coming into my mind. It kept whispering to me that I had to trust Him again. The voice told me that I belonged to God; and although I had given up, God hadn't given up on me.

I really wanted to understand, but how could my finite mind understand the infinite wisdom of God? As I wrestled with the thoughts, the voice inside me kept speaking, "Just trust me, just trust me." Repeatedly, it filtered into my spirit and my mind until I became encased by the thoughts. However, the anger was in the background, shouting that He had let me down. There in the darkness, another voice was speaking, and it was railing against the thoughts of God.

I knew then and there that I was in a battle for my soul. Satan had taken his chances to get me to deny God, just like he tried in the book of Job. I saw myself as Job and pictured the devil and God talking in heaven about me. I began to question if I was really that important? Who was I to God? And why did He choose me for this purpose? I concluded that I would not let the enemy have any victory, so I fell on my face before God one morning. I told Him that I didn't understand any of this and that I was still angry and scared. From the pit of my heart, I told Him how I really felt as the tears flowed out like rivers of water.

As I lay there sobbing and weeping with great force, I took a moment to pause. It was as if my soul had said, "That's enough." I pulled my thoughts together, and in those last few utterances before the master of my soul, I told Him, "I trust You, God, even if I don't understand. I trust You and Your will for my life. Your will be done Lord."

Those words rang in my ears as my mind was transported back to the Garden of Gethsemane. There I was with Jesus on the night before His betrayal, imploring God to take the cup away. The scriptures say that He prayed so hard that He literally sweated drops of blood. The thoughts and the anguish were so intense because He knew what He was about to face. In that moment, I wondered if he faced the thoughts of fear, doubt, and anger. The scriptures state that He did ask God to remove the cup from Him, but He went on to deny His own will and accept the will of God.

This passage lets me know that it was okay to question God and His ways. So that's exactly what I did. I asked Him, why did I have to pay such a huge cost? Why did His will for me come at the expense of losing the greatest part of my life? Kenisha was my victory over all my past failures. I had been in two disastrous marriages prior to meeting her. At one point, I wondered if marriage was for me. I never thought that I would be married three times. "The third time's the charm" was a phrase that we would laugh about all the time.

Kenisha truly loved me and her love was amazing. She made me feel like I was on top of the world. I realized that all the hell that I had gone through to get to her was worth it because she showed me what love was all about. Couldn't there have been another way? God, I did not deserve this punishment.

Suddenly, I heard a voice that said, "Oh, so you think that you don't deserve this? Well, let me ask you, did My Son deserve to die for you and everyone else in the world? What did He do to deserve the cross? Didn't He have to pay a huge cost for your salvation?"

This chastisement brought me to a place of humility. My sacrifice paled in comparison to the sacrifice that Jesus made for us. In that moment, I knew that God was showing me something, but I was not seeing it clearly. However, I did understand that His love for us was greater than any love that I could offer. I didn't have to go to the cross in order to save Kenisha or myself. It was already taken care of on the day of Christ's resurrection. Our debt was paid in full, and that was a fact. He was blameless, yet he took the blame for me and her so that we could be free.

Kenisha was not with me, but she was safe in His arms. I just had to realize that I was also safe. He was there with us in every moment, and He could not be taken away. Death may have taken Kenisha away from me for a moment. In time, I will see her again. But one thing is for sure: Death can never take Jesus away from us because He defeated death once and for all.

When we are faced with life's most difficult challenges, it is the nature of a man to rise and fight. It is programmed in our DNA to meet the threat head-on and attack it until we are victorious. It is easy to fight our natural fleshly enemies, but how will we react when our battles are not carnal? Spiritual warfare is something that I have come to be well-acquainted with since her passing. Most Christians have a faint understanding, but those that are truly called will be intimately intertwined with spiritual battles.

> Even though he kills me; I will hope in Him. Nevertheless, I will argue my ways to His face. (Job 13:15 AMP)

> Even though I walk through the valley of the shadow of death, I will fear no evil, for You are with me, Your rod and Your staff, they comfort me. (Psalm 23:4 ESV)

In this passage of scripture, the psalmist talks about walking through the valley of the shadow of death. Contemplation of this passage during my time of grief has brought me to some profound conclusions regarding grief and loss. I had always thought that this passage referred to when a person dies. They did not have to fear because death could not harm them. However, I believe that this passage also speaks to those that are left behind by their loved ones.

When Kenisha died, I felt like a part of me died as well. As my mind would flash back to memories of her home-going service, I saw myself lying in that casket with her. There were times when I even asked God why He didn't take both of us. Without her, I was ready to die, and for a time, I felt like I was one of the walking dead.

The days and nights ran together in an endless array of sorrow and darkness. I felt trapped between the grave and life, for I neither considered life nor death. It was as if I was paralyzed and unable to move. Both my mind and body were on autopilot as I made my way through the days. Time became irrelevant, and at some point, I stopped knowing what day it was. I would have to look at the calendar often just to know the day and the date.

At one point, I thought I had slipped into a pit of insanity. On numerous occasions, I wondered if this is what happened when a person went crazy. Yes, I felt like I was dead inside and out, but somehow, my body was still able to function.

One day, I came across Psalm 23, and it began to speak to me in a way that I had never heard it before. The fourth verse leaped off the page at me. As it spoke to my heart, I heard the voice of the Lord calling me back to life. Yes, I was in the valley of death, but it was just the shadow that blocked my vision. When she died, a part of me died as well, but my body and mind remained. I was wounded and scared because I had never faced this type of attack. The enemy took an occasion to deceive me into thinking that he had destroyed me and taken me down along with my wife. But the scripture states that it was just a shadow and it could not harm me.

I had to realize that I was still alive amid the darkness that covered my sight. It would have been so easy to just lie there and let it take ahold of me, but the small tiny spark inside of me would not allow it. Instead, I was reminded of scripture passages that seemed to flood my mind right when I needed them the most. Like the valley of dry bones, I began to prophesy over my situation and my mind. I wish I could tell you that it was easy, but it was an intense fight that the enemy waged against me.

The shadow was relentless. Once you are in its claws, it does not want to let go. It has a score to settle since it was defeated by Christ on the cross, and because of this fact, we can be assured that we have victory as well. Shadows always seem so ominous and foreboding, but we need not worry because it is just an illusion. You see, shadows are formed because an object does not allow light to travel through it. As the light travels around the object, it makes it appear larger than its true scale.

Light can never be stopped no matter what. However, we should not focus on the shadow or the object. Instead, we should always focus on the light. In that moment, I had to turn from the shadow so that I could see the light. However, the shadow of death is quite huge, so it wasn't possible to turn from it. I had to seek the wisdom of God in order to defeat this enemy.

In my inquiry, all I heard was the word *elevate*. Now I had to take a moment to figure it out, but like a lightbulb moment, the answer came to me. I had to elevate my mind and my position in order to see the light. In the darkness of the valley, God was there with me. I was in a valley, but the light was calling me out of the valley. The only way out was up, so amid the darkness, I started to climb. My progress was slow and treacherous at times, but I had to persevere.

Sometimes it felt like I was not making any progress, while other times, it felt like I had slipped and fallen back. But one thing that I was assured of is that God was with me in that darkness. I could not see the way, but I knew that he knew where to take me. I could feel His presence and hear His voice telling me to keep going forward and don't look back. However, the shadow was still nipping at my heels, trying to drag me back down into the depths of darkness. I could feel its icy hands trying to grab ahold of me, but I did not look back.

As I climbed higher and higher, the shadow began to lose its grip, and I could no longer feel its claws. The air was getting lighter, and I could see that my climb was nearing its end. The cliff was just a few feet away, and my heart began to rejoice. As I made it over the edge of the cliff, I lay there, panting, trying to catch my breath. Weary and bloodied by my climb, I slowly rose to my feet and looked out over the valley. With a great shout, I proclaimed my victory!

> O death where is your victory? O death
> where is your sting? (1 Cor. 15:55 ESV)

THE RIVER OF GRIEF

My short-lived victory over the shadow was not the end of the battle. Unfortunately, the war had just begun, and I was not prepared for what was to follow. I had to realize that I was on a journey toward something. What it was, I really didn't know, but after my long climb out of the valley, I knew that I could not stop to rest. Grief has a way of turning you on your head and making you question everything about your very existence. At times, I wondered if it would have been better to stay in that valley, rather than constantly exposing myself to the incessant barrage of my emotions.

Remember, I'm a man, and we don't handle emotions very well. We operate on logic and understanding, which has been intricately woven into the DNA of all men. It is our nature to analyze and conclude whether we should adapt or overcome what is before us. However, I found myself aimlessly wandering about as if my steps were being controlled by some unseen force. Logical thought had ceased, and my mind was awash in a hurricane of emotions that were whipping me and spinning me all around. I felt like Dorothy as she was caught up in the twister that transported her to that mythical place called Oz.

My mind was trapped in the storm, and I knew not where it was taking me. As I stopped to get my bearings, I noticed that I was standing before this great river. There I was perched on the shores, surveying all that was before me as logic tried to reason with my mind as to how I came to this place. In my mind, I sensed the leading of that unknown force that brought me here, and I wondered if this was a necessary part of the journey. There was nowhere to turn and nowhere to seek shelter. It was only instinct that told me that this was my way toward handling or hopefully overcoming my loss.

The river seemed calm. However, I knew that water can be quite deceptive in its invitation because you never know what's lurking beneath. How deep, how swift the current, and what the temperature was all came to my mind as I looked over the water. I wondered if I was to try to make it to the other side and how I was to do that, seeing that there were no boats around. The other side seemed a great distance off. I contemplated the odds of me attempting to swim, but I wondered if I could make it before the current had swept me down the river. Still, I felt the leading of that force that was nudging me forward into the shallows.

Like the sirens of the seas, the water beckoned to me its melodic invitation. I could hear the voices calling from the depths to get in. The hypnotic trance of tranquility danced through the recesses of my mind. I gave no resistance to the invitation, and somehow, I felt at peace entering the water. It was cool to the touch as I felt it climbing up my legs to my waist. As I reveled in the peace of the shallows, the voice of the force that was leading me began to speak within my mind. The voice sang its siren song of what was to come in the river and what I would have to go through in order to make it. It gave me hope that once through, I would be able to accept my journey and go on to live once again.

However, some of the stages sounded deep, dark, and dangerous to my state of being, and I was more than concerned that I may not make it. The voice spoke of denial, anger, depression, and bargaining before I would be allowed to journey to acceptance. It then warned me that the stages were not one after another because the ebb and flow of this river had the power to turn me in circles. The currents of anger and bargaining had the ability to come and go as they pleased. One minute, you could feel at peace; and then the next minute, the swirling current would pull you down into the depths of great anger.

Yes, this river was really treacherous. The voice made me question whether or not I should attempt to go through this process, but I knew that there was no way around it. Why did I need acceptance when my mind wanted to retreat to some faraway land where no one could bother me? If I accepted the fact that Kenisha was gone, would that make my life less painful? That was a tough pill to swallow. I also knew that depression alone had taken many souls who encountered its attack.

It is a stealthy assassin that has the ability to take you by surprise at any given moment. It can also just wear you down over time and make you give up. Also, most forms of depression required some form of drug therapy to overcome the attack. I am not a big fan of taking prescription drugs because I am afraid of side effects and getting hooked on them. In any case, I was more than a little concerned about battling depression.

Anger is one of the worst spirits to endure and fight with, and it has the power to make us go from sound judgment to utter stupidity in the blink of an eye. Many have been killed by the deceptive nature of anger, and once it is unleashed, there is no taking it back. Anger can be very volatile. One moment, you can be fine; and the next moment, it's like ten Hiroshima bombs just rained down on your position.

I do not like being angry because I try to keep peace in my life. I had already experienced a lot of anger when Kenisha passed, so I didn't want to relive any of those experiences.

I always knew that death was a possibility on this journey, and in some ways, I welcomed it if it would give me a chance to see my beloved once again. I was no longer afraid of death, having looked it straight in the eye when it took Kenisha away from me. I was ready to meet it head on and laugh in its face because I knew that it could not defeat me. Standing there in the shallows, I roared at death and proclaimed my strength and my ability to defeat the foul enemy of my body.

Yes, I was truly prepared to battle once again. My adrenaline was pumping full throttle through my veins while the thoughts of payback surged in my heart. I wanted to meet my enemies head-on and slay every last one of them. How dare they come against me and try to destroy my life!

I dove in and began to swim for what I thought was the other side. There seemed to be no resistance at the time as I would periodically stop to get my bearings. Wading in the deep of the river felt good after climbing out of that valley, and I took a moment to think that maybe I was through the worst of it and the rest of my journey would be easy. Whenever the thoughts of her loss would try to invade my mind, I felt myself deflecting my feelings. I tried to convince myself that I was in some cruel dream, and soon I would awaken to a beautiful day next to my beloved.

"Wake, up Eric, it's just a dream" is what I hoped to hear as I awakened to her smiling face. Or I would think that I was in a coma in the hospital and this was all just a mere consequence of my traumatic injuries. I really tried to focus on not thinking about the loss, and the waters of denial helped me to take my mind off the pain. I basked in the cool of the currents and took in the feel of the water washing over me. For the moment, denial was great because it was my hiding and resting place.

I didn't have to face reality, nor did I have to think about the loss. Whenever thoughts of pain tried to invade, I immediately reasoned that my feelings were the result of something other than the loss of my wife. It is amazing how your mind can come up with plausible excuses to deflect the truth. However, my mind would not relent to the denial. It's as if it had access to the master override command.

Soon, I found myself trying in vain to shut down all outside forces because I wanted to enjoy my self-made playground and not be paralyzed by my emotions.

At some point in time, I noticed that I was far away from the shore, and the water was deep and cold. The current was picking up, and off in the distance, I could see the jagged rocks popping out of the water. The rocks were dangerous, and I knew that they had the ability to rip me to shreds. I tried to change my course and swim away, but my helpless body was caught in the current, and I was unable to get out of their path.

I cried out as grief swept me away, tumbling me over and over like a rag doll caught inside a wave. The pain of the loss of Kenisha was at the forefront of my mind once again. The covenant that we made was now made void by her death. Death is the only thing that can end a covenant, and it is interesting that making a covenant involves the cutting of flesh. In our covenant, we became one—one heart, one mind, one spirit operating under God.

When she died, we were no longer one, and this process reversed itself as I felt her being ripped away from me. I was no longer whole. My other half was torn from me, and the pain of that process gripped my mind as I tumbled down the river. How could I survive and live being only half of a person? How could I love again? Because I felt like my heart had been ripped from my chest. I was no longer a man. I was a freak that you see in the carnival shows. I could hear the carnival barker saying, "Come see the amazing half man as he struggles to live!"

My mind was awash with thoughts of being whole again. What did that look like? And how could it ever happen? Or was I doomed to live out the rest of my life in this state? What did the future hold? I felt hopeless and out of control. As the waters took me deeper and deeper, I felt myself gasping for air. At one point, I just wanted to let it take me. I wanted to give in and just be swept away. However, I felt a hand lift me from the depths.

As I came to the surface, I gasped for a breath, and at that point, I noticed a rock that I could cling to. I was still in the river, but this rock was my resting place for a moment. At some point, I would have to let go and continue my journey, but for now, I was content to catch my breath and try to get my mind back together. The ripping and tearing of my flesh was painful, and as I hung on to that rock in my wounded state, I wondered if I would make it to safety.

I was in the middle of this huge river, and there was no way out. I couldn't swim to the sides because the current was too strong. I knew that the minute that I let go of that rock, my journey would begin again. I was afraid to let go, but I was cold and tired. My wounds were aching, and I needed the loving attention of my beloved Kenisha, but she could no longer soothe me. I cried in anguish as I recounted her loss and how helpless I felt. Kenisha was my rock, my reason, and my fortitude. Without her, I was doomed to be a shell of my former self.

I wondered in those moments if I could ever go on as I struggled to keep my grip on those slippery rocks. I could no longer feel my hands or my fingers due to the icy water making them go numb. The force of the water was now beating against every part of my body like a heavyweight fighter pummeling me against the ropes. I tried in vain to hold on, but I was torn away from the rocks by the cruel and cold waters of doubt.

The current was violent and relentless in its attack. My mind was filled with thoughts of failure and despair. I failed to save her life. I failed to get her the care that she needed. I failed to defeat the enemy that destroyed my kingdom. *You failed, you failed, you failed*, rang like school bells through my mind. The hot stinging whip of failure lashed upon my body with furious blows. Beaten and bloodied, the doubt continued to pummel me into the dust.

I questioned God, I questioned my relationship with Him, and I questioned my salvation. Was I really His child? Or was I just kidding myself for all these years? Did God really love me? And if He did, then why didn't He save her and keep us together? I had spent countless hours in church laying upon the altar in prayer, seeking Him for my destiny. Yet He never revealed to me that my destiny involved the loss of my beloved and the destruction of my life. Maybe He did try to tell me, but in my mind, I justified the fact that God would never allow me to suffer this fate.

God was good and loving, or so I thought. It would have never entered my mind that He would allow such a thing to befall me. Why me? What did I do to deserve this fate? All of this caused me to slip away from prayer and worship. Months after the funeral, I sat in church as a lifeless shell of a man. I tried my best to smile on the outside, but I was a mess on the inside. I had to keep a lid on my emotions so as not to arouse suspicion or inquiry.

I felt myself erecting barriers to all those around me in the sanctuary because I did not want deal with their questions as to my well-being. Quite frankly, I was tired of explaining how I felt and I was tired of giving the same responses over and over. I was only going because it was like autopilot in my DNA.

Sunday after Sunday came, and each time, I sat there and stared into space. As the choir sang, I sat there and stared at the place where Kenisha lay on the day of her funeral. It was imprinted upon my mind, and I could not erase the tape. The sanctuary had become my tomb of tormented thoughts. It was no longer a place of God's presence. Instead, it became a place where our lives had ended. So each time I entered the building, I could feel my mind drifting away.

I could not tell you what the choir sang nor could I tell you what the preacher spoke about. His pontification of the scriptures caused me to rebel in my heart, and inside, I felt my spirit smirking at his words. "God loves me!" the preacher would boast. I highly doubt that given the circumstances. If this was love, I wanted no part of it. It felt more like punishment and hate, rather than love. As I thought on it more and more, my mind pushed me further from God's truth. Doubt had me in its grips, and I was no longer thinking straight. I'm pretty sure that there were those around me who questioned my salvation at the time as well. They probably saw my confused and sarcastic looks that ran over my face as I sat motionless in the service.

In the depths of doubt and denial, the silence was deafening, and in that silence, it unleashed more attacks upon my soul. Anger was now coursing through my veins. Like a massive dose of heroin that incapacitates a dope addict, I was now under its control. My body was filled with the putrid stench of hatred and rage. At this point, the water was no longer consoling. On the contrary, I cursed the water and everything around me. I was at anger's mercy, and it was a force to be reckoned with because the slightest annoyance sent me into a rage within my spirit. It was as if the three forces were working simultaneously to destroy me.

As anger was working, I would begin to deny my feelings, which seemed to help control the rage for a time. I assumed I was okay, but anger and depression came back with a vengeance. I felt like a yo-yo that was being jerked back and forth through my emotions. Confusion reigned within me, and the only thing that I knew to do was cry out. As I continued my journey down the river, my mind was racing through all the events that had taken place in such a short period of time. In six short months, my life would crash and burn right before my eyes, and I could not do anything to stop its evolution.

I went from a life of happiness and joy to a life filled with misery, fear, and pain. The woman that I loved more than my life itself had died right before my eyes. Cancer had snuck in and taken ahold of her body. There were no warnings and no symptoms that would have alerted us to the impending doom. My internal security system had failed to alert me of the danger that was coming to harm me. I was angry with the failure and I was angry with the attack.

I searched my memory and found not one clue as to what had overtaken us. One minute, we were enjoying a vacation in an exotic destination; the next, I was being told that my wife had a year at best to live. It all came at me so fast that I was unable to handle the shock and confusion that ran over me like a semitruck barreling down the freeway. My life was turned upside down, and all I wanted to do was make it stop. Death forced me to drink the bile that it served up. I was forced to go through the merciless fire of losing my queen.

The trial of Meshach, Shadrach, and Abednego going into the fiery furnace is well-known to all Christians, but most of us have no clue of what it really means. My mind wondered what it must have been like to see that furnace and how they must have felt before going in. Were they all in agreement with Daniel's confession? Or did they have some small amount of doubt? As they walked up to the furnace and felt the heat, did they consider the possibility of death and what it would feel like? Did they feel the heat intensifying upon their skin as they got closer and closer to the fire? I'm pretty sure that a host of thoughts must have run through their minds, and they most likely felt the grip of fear coming over them.

In church's all across the globe, we shout every time the preacher talks about their victory, but what about the before rather than the after? Did they really want to go through this trial? I know this feeling because I had to take ahold of a cross that I never thought about bearing. It would have never entered my mind that God would put me through such a trial. However, here I was, being swept down a river that I never wanted to enter. I tried to hold on to God, but I felt like God didn't hold onto me. The voice in my mind questioned God again and again, yet He remained silent. I felt like I was owed an explanation as to why He allowed this defeat to overtake me. It was my right to question Him, and as I floated in the silence, I began to demand that he address my inquiries.

Alone and vulnerable in this cold murky river that was seeking to take me deeper and deeper into its depths, the questions weighed heavily upon me. Where there was once light, all I could see was darkness. My soul was sinking lower and lower into a deep abyss of darkness and despair. There was no way out, and I could not get my bearings, so I didn't know which way to swim.

It was frustrating and disconcerting to be in this position. Helpless and wanting answers, I couldn't comprehend the magnitude of my situation. Why me, Lord? Why did I have to bear this cross? My mind struggled to find the answers in the darkness, yet You have been silent to my pleas. Where are You? I have tried so hard to hear You, but all I hear is silence and all I feel is pain. Maybe I can't hear You because the anger inside of me drowns everything else out.

Like the pounding heartbeat of a runner, the anger beat against my chest. Numbing my senses, leaving me lifeless as I was sucked deeper and deeper into despair. Yes, I am angry! I wasn't just mad. No, this was raw uncontrollable rage! It was hot and searing in its intent, and it knew no boundaries, nor did it make any apologies. Like a bomb, it could explode with full force at any given moment.

I wanted this nightmare to end its assault upon my senses, but there was no end in sight. Longing for relief from the pain, I cried out for help to no avail. This was hell in all its misery, and the more that I struggled against it, the more that I sank into its pit. As I floated in the darkness, I was consumed with my thoughts and emotions. My mind became my enemy because all it could do was replay the horrific dreams of my loss.

I began to search back over the details of how I came to this place. In my thoughts, I looked for reasons to blame everyone and everything that played a part in this tragedy. At this point, I had realized that I had sunk into the deep abyss of anger. My anger knew no boundaries as it laid blame to anyone or anything that my mind focused on. I was angry with the doctors who couldn't save her. Did they really provide her with the best care or were they just in it for the money?

As I look back, I can remember that her primary oncologist left the country for almost forty-five days to visit his family. During that time, we were placed in the care of one of his associates. I always felt like he really didn't care enough to do anything special for my wife. After all, she was not his patient, so why should he go against his colleague. He was just a babysitter at best in my mind. So I tried to excuse him from my tirade, but as I thought about it more and more, I concluded that he was equally to blame.

He was a doctor who was supposed to be concerned with saving people's lives. Especially those who were dealing with such a deadly disease. Why didn't he intervene and prescribe another treatment? It really made me wonder if any of them really cared about the patients or if they just cared about the money.

In six months, my wife's medical bills totaled a staggering 1.5

million dollars. I saw all the bills that went to the insurance companies, and I was amazed at how much things cost. It made no sense to me that they could charge so much, especially after doing my research about her treatment protocol. They were charging thousands of dollars for medications that had been around and in use since the 1950s. I guess they figured that they could charge whatever they wanted because you have to ask yourself, what is your loved one's life worth? I guess you would pay anything to have them healed, so what if it cost that much? After all, they were billing the insurance companies, not me.

Yes, we had some co-pays, but many of the bills went to insurance. They rode the gravy train as long as they could until they finally concluded that they had done all that they could. At that point, they gave me the sad look of concern and despair, but I knew that they had given up when they referred her over to another cancer specialist. By the time we got to see the new doctor, it was too late. There was nothing that could be done.

As I heard those words, I could feel my anger rise inside of me because the other doctors knew this, but they were cowards who passed the responsibility off to someone else. This really made me want to scream at all the doctors who let my wife die. If I could exact any amount of vengeance upon them, I would have gladly done so.

I held them all personally responsible and wanted them to suffer just like me. They needed to know how they played a part in destroying my life. My thirst for vengeance was uncontrollably strong! In my heart, the anger pulsed, and at one point, I thought that lashing out at them would make me feel better. But I came to realize that they were not the ones who had the final say on whether she lived or died. They were insignificant cogs in the machine at this point, so I chose to leave them be.

However, every time I passed by their offices, I wanted to stop in and just look them in the eye to see if they truly cared about my loss. I wanted them to see the pain and anger that they produced. They gave me all this hope that they could save her life, but in the end, they could do nothing. They got my hopes of recovery up with all their slick commercials and marketing campaigns that made me believe that they had the best treatment plans. It makes me wonder why they didn't try other options. Why didn't they use the latest immunotherapies that they kept singing about? Where were they when she was struggling to survive? It made me sick every time I thought about it.

As I have stated before, the doubt caused me to blame myself for not saving her. I was angry with myself because I kept fighting the feelings that maybe I didn't do enough to help her survive. I was helpless, and I knew there was nothing I could do, yet the guilt and the doubt still haunted me. From time to time, my mind often wonders if it would have turned out different, if I could have gotten her to another doctor.

I had researched all these cancer clinics that talked about great success rates in fighting the disease, but the cost was too great, and our insurance didn't cover out of state doctors. Most doctors wanted deposits ranging from twenty-five thousand to fifty thousand dollars just to do an initial consultation. I contacted a well-known cancer treatment center that was supposedly known for caring about their patients as well as their families. Of course, they didn't take our insurance, but they still wanted to help us. I thought that this was great, and I prepared to give my wife the good news. That was until the person on the other end of the phone asked me for a $250,000 cash deposit just to see her for the initial exam. Talk about a kick in the teeth! I could not believe that they would ask someone for that much money up front, but they didn't flinch.

So once again, it boiled down to money. I began to see that this disease was all about making more money and not about helping people to survive. I tried my best to raise the money that was needed. We put on fundraisers and posted a GoFundMe page to solicit donations. The people were very generous, but we fell short of making our goal. At that point, I even considered robbing a bank to get the money, but I was never cut out for prison life.

Again, the anger inside of me intensified to the point of becoming an inferno. I couldn't control where it was taking me. This abyss was cruel and unforgiving. I would have never thought that I would ever have sunk to the depths I sank to. As the anger kindled inside of me, I found myself blaming God for all my troubles. In the deep sweeping current of darkness, I shouted that I was indeed angry with God. Yes, you read that right, I was angry with God! I lashed out at Him on several occasions whenever I tried to pray or read His Word. It was as if I was standing before Him, unleashing a volcanic eruption of emotions.

The virulence of my speech was sharp and caustic as I railed against everything that was associated with God. *Why did You let her die? Why didn't You answer my prayers? Our church was known for all these great testimonies of how You delivered, healed, and opened doors for your people. Why didn't You do it for me? I really thought that You would show up. We both believed that one day, we would lay the church out with a great testimony of how you healed her. The doctors said she had a year to live, but we believed in what Your Word said. We quoted scriptures day and night and prayed endless prayers, pleading for You to heal her.*

The entire church prayed for her, and my bishop spent hours at the hospital rehearsing confessions with her. We played gospel music 24/7, and the only thing we spoke on was her healing. We only allowed positive people that were full of faith to visit her. I had strict orders to keep those away that were not in agreement for healing. Even when the doctors would tell us otherwise, we put on a united front. We were primed and ready for the battle, and we could not be stopped.

It was as if I had amassed an army of faithful warriors that were ready to battle at a moment's notice. Cancer was a defeated enemy that tried to invade our home, but we would laugh in its face and stop it in its tracks. Little did I know that I was the defeated one. Cancer was the winner, and all my faith and beliefs were destroyed the day she closed her eyes. *God, You failed me. How can this be? I've heard it countless times that You can never fail. So please tell me what happened this time? You let me down. I believed in You and everything Your Word said, so why didn't it work for me? The heaviness of my loss crushed my spirit. Why me? Was Kenisha not worthy of saving? What did I do to deserve this? Please, God! Can You tell me why this had to happen? I don't understand any of this.*

Kenisha was my redemption and my triumph over years of bad decisions. She was my good thing and the love of my life. Kenisha was the victory after previous attempts of marriage failed. You told me to marry her, but You failed to tell me that our marriage would be short-lived. We didn't get to have a long happy life filled with children and great memories. Premature death never entered my mind because I thought that I was supposed to be the first one to transition due to me being the oldest. I always thought that I was going to provide her with a good life after I was gone. This was not the plan I had in mind. You could have healed her, but You chose not to save her. With one flick of your pinky finger, You could have destroyed every cancerous cell in her body.

Kenisha was Your child, and she believed that You would heal her. But You allowed death to take ahold of her. She was your prayer warrior who prayed incessantly for others to be healed. You answered her prayers for them, but You would not lift your hand to heal her.

Instead, I had to sit there and watch her die, which was the cruelest punishment. Helpless and powerless, I became a spectator in some cruel horrific movie that was playing out right before my eyes. It was like being in a nightmare that you knew was a dream, so you purposely try to wake yourself up before the horror overtakes you. However, as much as I tried, I couldn't wake up.

Like most men, I wanted to fix the problem, but this issue was beyond my scope. God, please know that I was really relying on You to come through, but You were nowhere to be found. Kenisha was once vibrant, full of life and joy. She had the most beautiful smile that resonated to the heavens, but now she was reduced to a lifeless shell. There were times when she was in so much pain that she winced with every movement. All I wanted You to do was take the pain from her and give it to me. I would have sacrificed my own life for hers because she was so special. If You wouldn't do it for me, I just knew that You would do it for her.

This is so hard to understand, and I have searched my thoughts over and over trying to come up with some explanation. Many have told me their opinions as if they knew what the answers were. I have tried to pray and listen for Your voice, but in this darkness and silence, all I hear is nothing. When I try to talk to You, I feel this intense anger flooding my body. The words are no longer audible as the screams of agony bellow from the depths of my soul. I'm left to my own thoughts, and my mind is flooded with sadness and grief.

You failed me God, and I am holding You responsible for my pain. How could You allow this? And why would You put me through this agony? In my anger, I no longer wish to be in Your presence. Please, just leave me alone to die in this dark hell that You created. I'm done trusting, believing, and praying. You are nowhere to be found, so I will walk this path by myself.

My mind was now ablaze in the fury of anger, and all rationality ceased to exist. The anger was in control, and I was its dog chained to a leash. As the yoke of anger pulled me down to my knees, I took one last look at God and told him to leave me. I was drowning in the depths of my anger, and I was content to let it take me because He wasn't there for me when I needed Him the most. *Was this payback for my many sins? Am I no longer worthy of Your love?*

My eyes were flooded with tears both day and night; hot and salty torrents of anguish falling from my eyes and watering my pillow as I relived the loss repeatedly. *I've cried out to You, but the silence is deafening. I really want to let go, but a tiny hope still resides within me. Maybe one day, You will forgive my anger with You, God. I'm sorry for being angry, but the pain of this loss is too great. Your Word says that you would not put more on me than I could bear, but this weight has crushed me. It feels like Mt. Everest has fallen on me, and I'm struggling to survive. I'm all alone now with no one to console me, and those that try don't have a clue of what to do or say. Most of them are other women who see this as an opportunity to strike and gain a prize. There fake concern for my condition and state of mind is easily seen through my lens of anger.*

Right now, the only thing that I can feel for another woman is the intense hatred I have for being in this situation. Every time I look at someone else, my heart pulses with feelings of rage and discontent. On the outside, I smile at them and maybe entertain their words; but on the inside, I scream and shout into the darkness of my soul where there was once light and love.

In this state, I'm defenseless and completely vulnerable. If there was ever a time where the enemy could strike, it would be now. He could easily take me out with one swift blow. Or he could use my anger to inflict damage upon anyone that stood in my way.

There were times when I wanted the enemy's weapon of choice.

I wanted to lash out at everything and everybody. One day, a motorist had cut me off in traffic, and I immediately chased them down. When I caught up with them, I felt the anger making me want to inflict harm upon them. Primed and ready for a fight, I wanted to lash out! Fortunately, my rage was quelled when I saw that the driver was an elderly gentleman. He probably didn't notice me or pay attention to his surroundings. He looked so innocent and clueless at the same time.

I sat back in my seat and knew that I was in trouble, but I was ready to give in to the darkness and let it take me down. I had finally come to accept that I was out of control and lost within my emotions. Helpless and defeated, I could no longer fight my feelings. In that moment, I knew that I was not okay, and in a weird way, the acceptance of this fact gave me peace.

A wave of humility engulfed my heart and my spirit as I shouted to God that I needed Him to save me from me. My soul began to thirst for His presence once again as I recounted the foolishness of my words and thoughts. Waves of repentance over all that I had said and done filled my mouth and spewed forth prayers asking for forgiveness.

It was at that moment, in the cold murky depths of that river, I suddenly felt a hand reach out for me. The hand reached down into the depths and pulled me up out of the water and lay me upon the shore. The disorientation of my experience prevented me from understanding who or what had just saved me from the water, but I was too cold and exhausted to concentrate or care. Once again, my mind drifted off, and in the distance, I could feel peace once again.

The anger had subsided, but the doubt still lingered in the shadows of my mind. In this comatose state, I heard the voice once again. It said that these feelings would always be with me, but in time, I would learn how to navigate them.

It reminded me of the Apostle Paul and how he asked God to remove the thorn from his flesh three times. In each instance, God said that His grace was sufficient. I knew then that whenever the feelings of grief presented themselves, I had the ability to overcome them through God's grace. His grace is more powerful than any emotion that can come against me. This thought alone brought me the rest that I sought.

As I came back to consciousness, I began to cry out and thank God for not giving up on me, even though I gave up on him. I bowed down to the heavens to offer up prayers of repentance once again. As I lay there on the shore before God and the angelic host, I noticed a beautiful sword and shield lying there beside me. The voice spoke once again and told me that these weapons were fashioned for my hand, but in my mind, I wondered if I was strong enough to pick them up. Was I ready to battle again? What if I were to lose again? I knew that I could not give fear a chance to deny my destiny, so I told God the truth about my uncertainty.

Maybe it was better to stay here than to journey on. However, the voice spoke like thunder from the heavens and told me to rise and recover. It spoke to my heart and gave me the strength and courage to continue. I was out of the river, but I knew that other battles were ahead of me. Plus, grief was still taunting me in the background, letting me know that it would never let go.

As I stood there in the darkness, wondering whether to cower in fear or journey on to another battle, I felt the anger begin to rise again. However, this anger was different in its intent. My anger was not focused on God or my loss; rather, it was focused on the enemy who came against my kingdom. I began to remember who I was and what I was called to be. The heart of a king was beating within me, and the warrior was ready to rise. The voice in my heart beckoned me to stand and fight!

This was truly a humbling moment as I fell to my knees before my creator. As I shouted out and asked for forgiveness for falling down, I could feel my heart and my mind accepting my fate. Years earlier, the Lord had come to me while in prayer and told me that I was going to be a "fisher of men." Back in those days, I struggled with this because I knew that men were some of the toughest individuals to talk to about God. I shied away from this responsibility, but now I found myself ready to accept the challenge.

All men should be prepared for battle because all men should see themselves as warriors. Battles do not come to destroy you, they come to make you into the image that God has of you. The loss was my gain, and in the midst of the expanse where I now stood, I could now begin to see a glimpse of God's plan. The river was behind me, and I was to journey forward and not look back. A centurion was being made and fashioned through this battle. God was with me, and I would not fear man nor spirit. My trust was predicated upon God and His word. It was time to live, serve, and fight for what mattered most.

The kingdom of heaven was my sole focus and not the scars of my battles. My scars are the testimonies of the power that lies within me.

> Little children (believers, dear ones),
> you are of God and you belong to Him
> and have [already] overcome them [the
> agents of the Antichrist]; because He
> who is in you is greater that he (Satan)
> who is in the world [of sinful mankind].
> (1 John 4:4 AMP)

Don't Say It

Over the course of my journey, I have concluded that people don't really know what to say to those that are grieving. Most people have good intentions, but even good intentions can have a negative impact on those that have suffered loss. So to help those of you who don't have a clue, please take note.

This chapter is meant to help you avoid looking like a fool or, at best, keep you from getting the side eye from those that are dealing with the pain and anguish of loss. If you have never been through a loss, you have no idea of the amount of pain and suffering that a person goes through. The grieving person is not on a linear journey that has a predetermined end. This is a journey that is filled with many highs and lows that are coupled with one step forward and fifty steps backward. Your attempts to identify will only serve to hurt the person even more or upset them to the point of rage.

Do not be surprised if the grieving person withdraws contact from you because they are probably concerned about your safety at this point. I am very serious when I say this because a grieving person is a ball of uncontrollable conflicted emotions. It is normal for those that are grieving to go from laughter to weeping in a matter of moments. Our emotional engines can go from zero to sixty in a matter of milliseconds, and the storm that will ensue is not pretty. It is best to let the grieving person be to themselves and calm down on their own. If you try to help or explain yourself, you will only make a bad situation worse.

Consider this a warning that you need to listen to and understand. Trust me, you don't want to dance with a grieving person during an emotional episode because the intensity can be quite damaging. If the grieving person is a God-fearing person, you will walk away, wondering if they have totally renounced God and all things holy. Don't be surprised at what comes out of their mouths. We will literally curse you out and then say "God bless you" afterward. The emotions are raw, and we make no excuses for our behavior. In fact, it is detrimental to our healing and our mental stability if we try to suppress anything that we are feeling, so please cut us some slack.

Now that the ground rules have been established, I have a couple of things on my list that were said to me that invoked pure thoughts of anger, hatred, and rage. Get it! These are just a few of the common ones, but there are hundreds of sayings that will push a grieving person buttons. Maybe you have said some of these in the past and thought you were helping. I can tell you right now that you weren't. You may not have noticed the look the person gave you or how fast they withdrew from the conversation, but I would bet any amount of money that the lightbulb is going to come on when you read these statements.

Because we were very active in the church, I often get people coming to me with words from the Bible about her being in heaven, rejoicing. And since I know this, I should also be rejoicing because she is with our heavenly Father. This statement makes me want to punch a person right in the face, and that's being kind because I really want to say a few choice words to them. Yes, I know where she is at and I know she is with God! But she is not here with me! How can you sit there and say that I should be rejoicing over her death? Have you lost your mind? You have no idea of the guilt, anger, and loneliness that I am facing! You don't know what it's like to come home to an empty house that was once filled with her presence and her laughter. You don't know what it feels like to look at photos and videos of her and weep over Kenisha not being by my side anymore.

Every moment now is a reminder that the person is gone. When I go to bed or wake up, I'm alone. Do you honestly know what it feels like to sleep in an empty bed where you once slept like spoons in a drawer? I don't hear her snoring anymore or complaining about she's too cold. Now I'm the one who is cold because I'm in a bed all by myself, reaching over to the side where Kenisha once slept and clutching nothing! You have no idea!

Or how about the fact that I can no longer visit the places we once called our special spots? Every time I pass by one of them, I am consumed by thoughts of my loss and how I can never go to that place with her again. Even the simple things like eating are now a chore because I eat alone. Cooking for her was one of my joys in life, and she loved the meals that I prepared. My work schedule allowed me to get home before her, so I was responsible for preparing dinner. She would come home from a hard day at the hospital, and her face would light up because I had dinner prepared.

I would greet her with a kiss and tell her to go and take a bath or shower to relax. When she got herself together, she would come down to the dinner table where I would serve her and pour her favorite wine. This was our time to relax and reconnect with each other. Kenisha would tell me about her day and some interesting moments at the hospital while I would gaze into her eyes and smile. God, I loved those moments! Now it's just me, and I no longer wait for her to come home. The table doesn't need to be set nor does the wine need to be poured. Dinner is no longer special. It is lonely and a stark contrast from the former things that made me happy.

It has taken me time to get used to this, and it is equally hard to go out to dinner by myself. There's no one to look at across the table nor share my day with. Sometimes I feel like I'm being watched by everyone. The spectacle of my loss and loneliness is there for all to see. Can they read my face and see my wounds? Or do they notice the withdrawn look in my eyes? Or can they sense the hurt and pain that I feel as I look throughout the restaurant and see all the couples enjoying themselves? It only reminds me of what I no longer have. It reminds me that I am alone and compounds the pain.

So please, for the love of God, do not patronize me with me your biblical quotes, thinking that it will be a source of comfort. You only make the situation more unbearable because you really don't understand where I am right now and you don't understand my feelings toward God. I am quite angry with God for allowing this to happen to me. We are not exactly on speaking terms at the moment, so the last thing that I need to hear is to rejoice. Saying this only serves to let me know that you are either clueless or you are a narcissistic fool that is only interested in making yourself look like you have garnered some deep revelation from God. Go sit down before I put you down!

And if all of this sounds too harsh, I apologize, but you really need to understand what you're dealing with. Once again, you have been warned!

The next on my list is no less revolting than the last. Let me start off by saying that I know you are trying to empathize with my feelings, but all you are doing is making me angry. So please do not try to tell me that you understand how I feel because your divorce was like death. Divorce can never compare to death. Yes, divorce is a devastating loss, but it is not a death of someone you loved and cared for. Please do not make any attempt to liken the two because you will get the death stare from the grieving person. You will get this look because we will be forced to tell you how you are wrong, which means we will have to go back and relive the situation all over again in order to provide clarity.

We are trying our best to avoid any reminders of our loss, and your misunderstanding of death and divorce forces us back into the dark abyss of anger. For the sake of argument, I will attempt to give you some insight into why the two are mutually exclusive. Let's start with divorce, which is a choice two parties or one person in the marriage makes because there is a breakdown in the covenant. Yes, it is a choice because you must conclude that you are no longer willing to live, build, and dream with your mate. However, your choices can be altered by several different courses of action. You can choose to go to counseling to see if your differences can be worked out or you can choose to attend workshops and retreats to work on your differences and build stronger bonds. You can also seek spiritual solutions and ask God in prayer to help you and your mate see eye to eye. These are just a few of many suggestions that can be used to help you maintain a lasting and loving relationship if you choose.

In some states, when you apply for divorce, they make you go through a cooling off period before the divorce is finalized. The most common time frame is six months, and it is designed to allow the anger and emotions to dissipate. Anger has a way of clouding judgment, so if it can be quelled, there is a chance that the couple will see that they can make it work and avoid the divorce. I hope that you are now getting a good understanding. But I know that you are probably thinking that none of those options worked and you still lost. Your marriage is done, and you are devastated with the fact that you must start over just like the person who experienced the death.

Before you throw up your hands and shout victory, please consider this last and final point on divorce. Even if your marriage ended one year, five years, or ten years ago, there can still be hope of a future reconciliation. I have witnessed couples that were ready to tear each other apart for years after their divorce concluded; however, a spark was still burning, and they realized that they still loved one another.

They realized their wrongs that brought them to the point of divorce, and they make the necessary changes to show the person that they have changed.

Yes, before you run off screaming and gagging, it is possible to change and come back together. The point that I am trying to make is that there is always hope and a chance that things can change. In divorce, you will always have a choice.

This is not the case with death. Death is not a choice, and it is *final!* There are no remedies or retreats that will cause the circumstance to change. Death is an absolute that none of us has any power over. It comes, it takes, and it destroys. There is no reasoning with it, there are no bargains to be made. You are forced to accept it and deal with the aftermath for the rest of your life. Death takes what you love and leaves you battered and wounded.

Kenisha and I were in love, and we never wanted to be apart from one another. We didn't decide to part, nor did we look at each other one day and say, "I hate being with you." Our goal was to live a long and happy life that was filled with children and family. Life with her was a dream come true until death came in and created the nightmare that I now have to deal with. Death didn't ask for permission nor did it give us fair warning. It didn't care about our feelings and the fact that one of us was going to be left behind to try to live on. No. Death just invaded our territory and took what it wanted.

We didn't go to a court of law to seek mediation or reconciliation. There were no lawyers fighting on our behalf, and there was no moment of throwing ourselves on the mercy of the court. A sentence was cast down, and we were left to deal with the outcome. Case closed!

Also, there is no coming back from death. God will not show up one day and say that He made a mistake. He will not send and angel to turn back time and right the wrong. There is no hope that I will ever see her on this earth again. It's just not possible.

I hope that you can finally see the error in your argument that the two are the same. After all that I have said, even Stevie Wonder can clearly see the difference. To those that are divorced, I am sorry that you think that your hurt and pain compares to mine. However, please refrain from further comparisons with those that are grieving because you may not like our response. You have been warned.

Another saying that makes me ill is when people try to tell me that she would want me to go on and be happy. Or they'll say that it's time to move on and rebuild. Both statements are very insensitive to a grieving person. I know that you mean well and that you are trying to get me out of my hole, so to speak. But once again, you are causing waves of anger and frustration to overtake me. How do you know what my wife wants me to do? Have you spoken to her? Do you have a direct line to heaven where you can speak to the dead and receive specific instructions? Please tell me how is it that you think you can speak on her behalf? What gives you the right to make such a cruel statement? How can I go on when my heart has been ripped out of my chest? How can I look at another woman and feel the same way?

Kenisha was one of a kind, and she was my everything. Kenisha was not perfect, but she was perfect for me. Now you come to me and try to tell me to move on and it's time to rebuild. Have you honestly looked at my life? It is as if a hundred nuclear bombs fell on top of my house and totally wiped out the area. So you say, "Rebuild!"

With what? There is nothing left! I've lost everything, and the earth around me is scorched! The blast and the impact have totally injured me, and my recovery is uncertain. Who knows how deep my wounds go and what it will take to heal? Your words cut deep and only serve to reopen the wounds that are trying to heal. So please just keep your thoughts to yourselves, and do not tell me what you think she would want.

And please do not tell me that time heals all wounds. Time is my enemy at this point because all I have is time—time to relive, time to reflect, time to grieve, time to weep, and a whole lot of time to feel the anger in my soul. Time does not heal this wound because this will always be with me. I will never forget this feeling or this great loss. Her smile is forever burned in my mind, and time is irrelevant when it comes to memories of her. Can anyone tell me how much time it will take for me to get used to her not being by my side? Or can you tell me how much time it will take to heal?

Time does not heal. It only gives you time to learn how to deal with your loss. The pain will lessen over time, and so will the grief, but the loss will always be with me. In the past two years, I have noticed that the memories of her don't cause me to go into fits of uncontrollable rage. I no longer cry and weep as much as I used to. However, I still have my moments of uncontrollable sobbing. I still cry whenever I think about Kenisha. It could be something as simple as the way she used to laugh or the fact that her snoring kept me from sleeping most nights. You have no idea how much I would love to hear her snore once again.

In time, I will be able to smile and reminisce about our love. One day, I will be able to love again. This will take time because my heart still belongs to her. A wise person once told me that I will have to find a way to keep my love for her tucked away in a special chamber of my heart. That way, I can reserve the other space for someone else. But of course, this will take time. How much time it will take is not my concern, nor should it be yours. You are not in charge of time, so please stop putting those that are grieving on a time clock.

When I lost Kenisha, it was as if time stood still—seconds into minutes, minutes in hours, hours into days, days into months—until I finally realized the amount of time that had passed. My mind struggled to comprehend where I was at, and I often questioned the day and date. I thought I was losing my mind, but I had to realize that time had stopped for me because it was the only way that I could stay sane. From her diagnosis to her transition was a mere six months, which went by very quickly as I look back. I wasn't able to handle the thoughts of what my life was going to be like in six months or a year. So in order to protect me, my mind shut time down.

Time is now irrelevant yet very precious to those that are grieving. It has to be irrelevant for us because we would drive ourselves insane if we could only redeem the time. So we have to let some aspects of time go in order to protect our mental stability. However, time is also precious because we now understand that we do not have the time that we think we have. We have come to learn to embrace each and every moment that we have.

Time is truly a mystery, and I could probably write whole books about the subject from my newfound perspective. But in the context of my argument, please refrain from reminding a grieving person about time. We will move and react in our own time and on our own schedule. It is not for you to dictate to us when we should do anything.

So you are probably wondering what you can say to those that are grieving. I know you mean well and your heart is in the right place, so let me give you a few pointers. These responses are the least confrontational and should steer you clear of any impending danger from the grief-stricken person. I know you are probably scratching your head right now, trying to figure out how your comments could be detrimental to your physical well-being. But trust me when I tell you that I and a number of those grieving a loss wanted to hurt those that tried to help us. I can only call it temporary insanity, but it's not intentional.

If you truly care about the person and what they are going through, your best response is to let them know that you may not understand what they are feeling with the loss; however, you want to be there for them in their time of need. You can let them know that it is okay to feel the way they feel and that when they are with you, they are safe. A safe zone for a person dealing with loss is crucial to their healing because they can't control their emotions and thoughts.

I know that when I was really in the thick of my grief that my emotions and my thoughts were all over the place. I know that some friends and family members thought that I had lost my mind, and looking back, I can certainly see why. But there were people in my life who took the time to cut me some slack and gave me some room to be crazy. They didn't judge and they didn't scold me for the stupid things I did. They offered their understanding of the situation and watched out for me so that I would not make a bad situation worse.

Grieving people need what I call insulators. At the beginning of this journey, we are not ready or equipped to handle what we are about to endure. This can cause a host of problems for those around us because they are not expecting our responses, and neither are we. We need insulators on our jobs, in our families, and in the church. Especially the church because most of my friends probably thought that I had given up on God and everything that was holy. Don't worry, I have not backslidden.

But seriously, empathy is a great tool when dealing with the fragile nature of a grieving person. Please don't try to tell them how to feel because you have no idea of how much pain they are in. It's best to tell them that you are here for them in any way, shape, or form. Tell them if they want to call you and scream or cry that it's all right. If they need you to listen, then give them that listening ear. Sometimes, we just need to release all of the pent-up emotions inside of us.

I know that is particularly true for men because we are not good with handling our emotions. Men are taught to show strength and not weakness. To a man, crying is a sign of weakness, so we tend to bottle it up until it explodes. I have been blessed with individuals who have allowed me to cry and release. It has been so comforting to be able to let go without fear of judgment. So to all my ladies who have lent their shoulders as catch basins for my tears, I say thank you. Hope Ellison, Alicia Graham, Karen Strasser and Niesha Harris—these are a few of my insulators that have helped me to cope with my loss. You all have been true gifts from God, and I want you to know that I could not have made it this far without you. Your kindness and your empathy helped me to see my journey in a different light. God used you to let me know that He was always there with me, and He will continue to provide what I need in every season.

It's also okay to say nothing at all to a grieving person. What I mean is it is okay to just give them a look of kindness and love. It's okay to grab them by the hand or give them a warm embrace. I can't tell you how many times this has helped me deal with the weights I was carrying. The heaviness of grief is overwhelming, and it feels like you're carrying an elephant on your shoulders everywhere you go. When those that were closest to me hugged me or looked into my eyes with a sincere look of compassion, it made me breathe a sigh of relief. If only for that moment, it allowed me to take off the weight and feel normal again.

We wear a lot of masks when we are grieving because we are tired of explaining ourselves to a world that does not seem to understand or care about what we are going through. We are tired of telling the story of how we became widows or of how we lost that special parent, sibling, or child. It is a narrative that we rehearse in our heads daily. We don't want to relive the drama, but for the sake of getting you to understand, we tell the story over and over, hoping that you will somehow view us in a different light. We hope that you will understand that we are not the same person that we were prior to the loss.

Grief evolves our spirit, our mind, and our social constructs. We will never be the same again, and we do not know who we are becoming. This is a new course heading that we were not prepared for nor were we given any warning. So yes, there are many times when I am smiling on the outside, but on the inside, I'm screaming and crying. It takes an immense amount of energy to keep those feelings bottled up and present the best picture to the world.

I had to try to keep myself together at work so that I could perform my duties. On most occasions, it was an immense struggle to smile when all I wanted to do was cry. So I would like to thank all those special people in my life who helped me along the way. You know who you are, but I must give a special thanks to my brothers, Ambassador Price and Jason. During my most trying moments, these men stepped in to keep me from going down to destruction. Thank you for insulating me and keeping me from going off the deep end. They made sure I didn't get into any trouble that would cause me to lose my employment. These brothers are the type of men we should all aspire to be.

Born Again

During my journey, a pastor by the name of Gerald Johnson sat me down one day and asked me how I was coming along? I listened to him intently because he too had experienced a tragic loss. His daughter was killed in an accident many years ago, and to look at him, you would never have known it. He was vibrant and full of life whenever I saw him. It was as if he had never suffered such a tragic loss.

As we talked, I noticed that he was looking at me as if he was peering into the deepest recesses of my soul. He listened and acknowledged my pain, but what he said next shook me to my core. He told me that I was lost in a fog of emotions and unable to see my way out, but one day, the sun would shine again. At the time, I was so deep in my darkness that I could not begin to think about sunshine. However, as I am sitting here, writing this book two years later, I can tell you that the clouds are beginning to part.

Yes, it has taken time to see the light in the midst of the darkness. My journey has been long and discouraging at times, but I now can see the light on the horizon. Don't get me wrong, there are still times of heartache and frustration. Whenever thoughts of Kenisha fill my mind, tears begin to flow. Yes, I still truly miss Kenisha with all my heart, and not a day goes by that she is not in my thoughts, but that is part of the journey. The sun will shine again and continues to resonate in my mind like the dawning of a new day. The light that I see is warm and inviting. It is increasing my hope and my faith that just like my friend who lost his daughter, I too can smile again.

I have often heard the saying that "God is no respecter of persons. What he does for one, he will do for another." If God has allowed my friend to feel joy once again, I will stand in expectation of the time when I can truly feel at peace. However, my understanding of grief is that it is a never-ending journey because Kenisha will always be with me in my heart. The deep-seated memories of our life and our love will forever be encased in that special place that is reserved for her. There is a place where only she resides, and in this place, she will never die.

The love that we shared is eternal and everlasting. Death can never sever a love tie because true love, like that displayed by the risen Christ, is eternal. Love is greater than anything, for it was empowered on the day that our Lord and Savior gave up the ghost to save us. It was love that allowed him to endure the most horrific tragedy known to man. It was love that kept him from calling legions of angels to save him from the pain of sin and death.

Yes, love is truly powerful and can never be defeated. I will love Kenisha for eternity, and I know that her love extends beyond the grave. I can feel Kenisha's presence and her warmth every time I think of her. I will journey on until my time comes to see her again. It is my sincere hope that she will be waiting for me when the time comes for me to cross the great threshold of death.

Yes, I long to see the face of my Savior, Jesus Christ, and all those that will have crossed before me. But I want to see that smile that made my heart melt so many years ago. I want to look into her eyes once again and feel the joy of her presence. I don't know what heaven will be like, but I sure hope that I will be able to see Kenisha again.

Through this experience of loss, I now have a better understanding of the sacrifice that Christ made for us on the cross. His mission was to seek and save the lost and the rejected ones of society, but in order to do so, he had to pay the great price. This price was so great that none of his disciples nor his followers understood what his mission entailed. There expectation was a triumphant victory over the forces that were against them; however, they were not prepared for what was to follow. They never expected to see their friend and their leader hanging on a cross, being mocked and ridiculed by the hordes.

Likewise, I never expected to have to endure the death of my beloved. Like the disciples, I was assured in my beliefs that everything was going to be all right and that we would win the battle. I now know how they must have felt on that day when they saw Christ on the cross. The scripture states that when he gave up the ghost, darkness overshadowed the earth. That same darkness is what overshadowed me in the valley. Great sorrow and mourning engulfed their souls as He lay in the tomb for those three days. The disciples were confused, scared, and lost like a rudderless ship listing in the storm, awaiting its peril.

Peter, his chief disciple, went fishing, and many others went into hiding. I can only imagine what was going through their minds at the time. Were they feeling doubt, confusion, anger, guilt, and grief? Did they question all that they knew or held onto like I did when my beloved died? Did they question themselves and lay blame upon each other for what had taken place at Calvary? And did they wonder if they could have done more to save their beloved friend?

Surely, they must have felt betrayed because they did not expect to be defeated and left behind. This was not the victory that they had imagined nor hoped for. But on the third day, the sun began to shine again. When the stone was rolled away from the tomb, Christ rose from the dead with all power in His hands. He had returned from the grave just like He said He would. The sun was shining yet again. The comfort of His presence overshadowed the pain of death and loss. We too must learn to stay in His presence if we are to ever make it through our brief moments of pain and suffering.

> In your presence is fullness of joy; at
> your right hand are pleasures forever
> more. (Psalm 16:11 ESV)

When Christ appeared unto His disciples in those following days, their hope, faith and strength was renewed. Their hearts and minds were enlightened with the truth of His words to them before He went to the cross. The scriptures states that Jesus appeared unto many over a forty-day period before ascending to heaven. During this time, He visited many to reassure them of His promises. As I think about this moment in time, I find myself longing for that length of forty days. I wish that my journey was that short, but I must remember that it makes no difference how long it takes.

God is not concerned or focused on time, so it is best to maintain a focus on the only one who can make the light shine once again. It could be three days, three months, or three years; however, He has promised to be with us until the end. He has promised us that the sun will shine again, and now I can fully understand my friend and the smile on his face when he told me this fact many days ago.

In the following weeks after her death, I could have never understood this because my mind and my soul were darkened by the pain of the loss. However, that small ember of hope had been smoldering within my heart all along, waiting for the time to ignite once again. Under the ashes of my loss, it flickered in the darkness, hoping for the fresh wind of the Spirit to breathe upon it. God's promises began to hover over it once again, and I could feel the warmth of the fire within as it began to burn. My mind remembered that Jesus was the promise that defeated both natural and spiritual death. This truth began to resonate in my heart, and I began to receive life-giving revelations once again.

As I stated earlier, the loss of Kenisha made me feel as if I was dead. A piece of my soul left with her, and I was left to try to go on. However, Christ left it on record that we must lose in order to gain. As I pondered this, I began to see Christ and myself in a whole new light.

It is interesting that Christ went to the grave beaten, bloodied, and weary. The stench of defeat was all over Him as He hung from the cross. However, during His tomb time, a great transition took place. He went in defeated, but He came out triumphant! He went into the grave in weakness, but He came out in power! Through this knowledge, I have received a powerful revelation and paradigm shift in my thoughts. My loss is producing great gain within me, for I now know Christ and the power of His resurrection! I too went into this battle and became beaten, bloodied, weary, and defeated. But Jesus left it on record, that this is the transition to power.

I am being transformed through this loss and I know not what I will become. But one thing is for sure. I know that I will be just like Him.

> And we know that for those who love God all things work together for good, for those who are called according to his purpose. For those whom he foreknew he also predestined to be conformed to the image of his son. (Rom. 8:28-29 ESV)

This is the glory of God. My loss is molding me into the image of Jesus Christ. And likewise, you too can praise God for your sufferings because this is the plan for all who claim the way of Christ. It has been left on record in numerous scriptures that this walk is the suffering walk, but it will eventually produce glory and praise.

Yes, suffering is not pleasant, and no one wants to suffer, but it is a crucial element of your destiny. The Apostle Paul left clear instructions.

> Indeed, I count everything as loss because of the surpassing worth of knowing Christ Jesus my Lord. For his sake I have suffered the loss of all things and count them as rubbish, in order that I may gain Christ and be found in him, not having a righteousness of my own that comes from the law, but that which comes through faith in Christ, the righteousness from God that depends on faith, that I may know him and the power of his resurrection, and may share his sufferings, becoming like him in his death, that by any means possible I may attain the resurrection from the dead. (Phil. 3:8–10 ESV)

This is the answer that I have been searching for over these years since Kenisha went home to be with the Lord. My mind can finally rest and be at peace because the Word of God gave me the understanding of how to deal with my grief. To most people, this will not make sense, but just know that this life is full of suffering.

The way to end suffering is through sacrifice. It is amazing to me that we all want to be like Jesus, but we don't want to suffer like he did. We want the glory without the grief. We want the muscles without having to go to the gym. These things do not make sense to me. However, what makes perfect sense is the fact that the road to heaven is paved with loss. You have to lose in order to gain. In short, we must lose ourselves and all that we desire in order to attain the glory of God. It's not about us. It's about serving God and being transformed into the image of Christ. Now my understanding is clear when Jesus made the statement in the garden, "nevertheless, not as I will, but as You will" (Matt. 26:39 ESV).

There is a common phrase that is talked about by those experiencing grief called "a new normal." In my new normal, I no longer feel the same way I did about life and God. The loss of Kenisha has given me a new understanding of my relationship with God and those that are around me. A new mission has been placed in my heart, and I am ready to get back into the fight.

Though I was down in the pit of destruction, I was never out of the game. The pit was supposed to be my grave, and I could hear the enemy screaming his victory over me. But I am reminded by the scriptures that we never understand the plans of God.

> What I am doing you do not understand now, but afterward, you will understand. (John 13:7 ESV)

Many experts on grief and loss have said that we must accept our new normal, but at times, I wonder what that will look like for me. This experience has changed me in so many ways that sometimes, I even question myself to see if I am all right. Some have even told me that I am not the same and that they are not sure of my path, but most of them are not concerned about my victory or my relationship with God.

Most of them have other intentions, both good and bad. However, my new normal is ever evolving, day by day. I am learning to trust God on every level of my life, and I no longer put so much emphasis on the trivial pursuits of this world. I am a man who loved a woman that was my life, and that life was all about her and how she made me feel. But I had to remember that I was a king who was charged with the welfare of his kingdom.

My calling to serve the kingdom was never negated by the loss of my beloved Kenisha. My loss was not for me; rather, it was for those that need to hear that they too can make it. My life is not my own, for I belong to one that is greater than me. I live to serve Him and to do all that He has commanded me to do. I now know that I am an instrument for His glory, which is being revealed in my tribulation and suffering.

> For I consider that the sufferings of this present time are not worth comparing with the glory that is to be revealed to us. (Rom. 8:18 ESV)

The ways and the will of God are enlightening my heart. Previously, I had faulted God for not being there when Kenisha died, but I had to realize that according to the scripture, God does take a moment to turn away from His children when death comes. I am reminded of Christ's own words on the cross when He asked the Father why He had forsaken Him.

Could this have been a precursor for all of us who would have to struggle with grief and loss? Was Christ letting us know that it is okay to feel doubt about God? Was it okay to question God as to why my plans didn't line up with His plans? I believe that this is exactly what Christ was trying to show us. Once again, it's okay to feel like God has abandoned you. Bible scholars have noted that at this very moment, Christ was fully human as God poured out the sins of the world upon Him.

During that moment, I can sense that Christ felt the pain of loss and grief. He knew what death produced in the lives of His children whom He loved so much. You see, He knew that death not only took the person, but it also had the ability to destroy those left behind to suffer the loss. As Jesus agonized and suffered every painful feeling on that cross, He knew He was setting us up for the ultimate victory. Jesus knew that He was giving us a way to know that Gods love is always there, and that just like His resurrection, we would see our loved ones again.

Yes, the sun will shine again. We are covered under the shadow of His mighty wing. We are hidden in His strong tower. He is with us in the silence and the darkness. We are never alone because He has sworn to protect us. This brings new meaning and fresh revelation to the fact that when we walk through the valleys of death, loss, and pain, we are never alone. When we want to question God about our pain, He is always listening. And in time, He will give us the power to understand or accept His will for our lives.

God can take every emotion that we can throw at Him and still respond to us from a position of love and healing. If only we would allow ourselves to open up and be 100 percent real with God, then He could lead us to a place of peace. When we hide our thoughts and true emotions from God, we don't give Him a chance to take our pain away. He is our father who stands in the gap, waiting to give and to restore.

I know that we have heard the phrase "Give it to God" many times, but sometimes, we don't know how to let go and surrender it to Him. It is really simple. All you have to do is keep it real. In my moments with God, I have cursed, screamed, thrown things, and told Him that I never wanted to walk with Him again. In all those heartfelt moments, I could hear him saying, "That's okay, Eric, keep giving me your pain, no matter what it sounds like."

God didn't smite me nor did He turn away from me during the ferocity of my anger. Instead, He turned toward me and wrapped me in His arms. When I was finished, He picked me up and told me to go on, and that was it. That's the love of God, and He wants to give it to all of us. Yes, beloved, it is that simple.

One day, while driving to work, the Lord brought me back to the dream I had the first night after Kenisha had passed, the one of the closed door. If you recall, I had a dream about a closed door, and all I heard was screaming on the other side. Death had come for Kenisha, and at that point, I was at my most vulnerable.

During this time, there was a great amount of spiritual warfare taking place in the spirit realm, and I believe that the dream was a glimpse of the battle that was being waged on my behalf. My weakened state made me ripe for the picking, and any demonic force could have overtaken me at that time. Those were the screams that I heard on the other side of the door. God was the door that kept me safe. He was standing between me and every evil entity that wanted to attack.

In the midst of my distress, it was hard for me to realize this fact because I was so weak and distraught. But now that I am coming out of the darkness, I can clearly see that God has been there all along. The darkness that surrounded me consumed me with doubt and anger. Destruction was before me, and I failed to realize that there was a war being waged against me. God was faithful, and He was true to His promise. Somewhere deep within my soul, His Word rang true. God will never leave me nor forsake me because I am His child.

When Christ said it was finished, He closed the door on anything that death could do to us. Death no longer has any victory, and the grave cannot hold us. We are shielded from demonic attacks that seek to destroy us when we are down. God knows our limits and our boundaries, and I can rest assured that He has me for the rest of my journey. We are free! Yes, we all must have a date with death, but it is a mere transition and not a sentence. We will face loss, but it is not the end. One day, I will see my savior and my beloved Kenisha again. On the other side of resurrection is where we will meet all of those that we have loved and lost in this life. We will be reunited with them to live out eternity, free from pain and suffering.

> And He will wipe away every tear from their eyes; and there will no longer be death; there will no longer be sorrow and anguish, or crying, or pain; for the former order of things has passed away. (Rev. 21:4 AMP)

ELEVATION

Although the loss of Kenisha was catastrophic, my mind has been elevated to higher thoughts and new levels of understanding. Like I said before, I have changed my outlook on so many things as it pertains to life and serving God. The death of my beloved had a cataclysmic effect on my flesh and my spirit. Something in me had to die as well in order to accept the will of God.

The phrase "dying to self" has taken on a whole new meaning for me. If you are going to walk with God, a paradigm shift is in order. The mission at hand is to produce more disciples, so I must now focus on community rather than self. To put it plainly, it is not about me or my will. It is about the will of God and His glory.

In the natural, we know that a seed is planted in the ground to reproduce after its own kind. A single seed has great reproduction power within it. We need only look at fruit for an example. Apples have seeds that produce trees, and these trees can produce hundreds of apples. But we also know that the seed cannot create the tree unless it dies after it has been buried in the ground. The seed must be transformed because it is not what's on the outside that makes the seed so powerful. The true power lies within the seed.

However, in order to get on the inside, the hard exterior must be broken down and weakened so that life can push its way out. It must be planted in the earth where darkness, pressure, water, and microorganisms work to extricate the life within the seed. Once the opposing forces have acted upon the seed, a powerful transition takes place within the earth. A new creation that looks nothing like the seed springs forth to take on a life of its own.

Likewise, Jesus was the seed that produced righteousness for mankind and saved us from death. He was planted in the grave for three days. During that time, the transformation took place, and the grave could no longer hold the power and the glory of what Jesus had become. He was a new creation that produced disciples that carried the seeds of life within them. And that same seed is continuing to produce other disciples to this very day.

So as you can clearly see, a seed is powerful. We should never underestimate its ability to transform the environment.

When I think on this, it gives me a keen understanding of what God wants me to do. The mission has come down from intelligence, and it must be fulfilled. The warrior in me has arisen, and I seek to do battle against the opposing forces of grief that seek to take others down. The Lord is giving me "beauty for ashes," for in those ashes, I am now able to see my way clearly.

Let my words flow from these pages and give you the promise of the oil of joy for those that mourn. I know that you don't understand His plans. I too was in the same position at the beginning, and there are still moments when I question the way. However, I am coming to the understanding that some things will never make sense and some things are being made clear as I journey on. It is imperative that we come to the conclusion that God is in control of everything.

How can we ever fully understand His thoughts or ways? For we each hold a purpose on this earthly plane, and when we take the cross upon us, we must ready ourselves to bear the full weight of its destiny. For we all must make our way toward Golgotha. It would be foolish of us to think that we could ever bypass the way and weight of the cross.

Yes, Christ took on the worst of it with His death, but we too must face our own transition. When He told Nicodemus that He must be born again, I believe that He was telling him that He would one day face His own cross to find renewal. I have come to the conclusion that the resurrection that was promised for the dead was not just for those who have transitioned physically. I believe that it is also meant for those that need to transition spiritually. For the Word of God states that we are to be transformed by the renewing of our minds so that we may be of service to God.

I have heard many preachers speak on this scripture and offer their thoughts of its meaning. Many have said that a renewing of the mind takes place by filling your mind with the Word of God instead of words of the world. While I will accept this synopsis of the Gospel, I do believe that renewal of the mind can also take place when one chooses to die to self and totally submit to God. In other words, something in us has to be crucified on the cross and put to death in order for renewal to take place. I believe that we all carry something that keeps us from truly fulfilling our purpose in this life. It is a shame that we allow the world to dictate our journey instead of our creator.

As stated before, we all must face the cross and we all must give an account of this life. God truly knows what needs to die in order for us to live the life that He intended. But we are too busy pursuing earthly treasures, rather than spiritual treasures. Ask yourself the question, "Am I really happy with the path my life has taken? Or could I have gone another way?"

Is fear of failure your motivation? Or are you driven by the need to succeed? Maybe these are the things that need to die. Only you and God know the answers.

These thoughts bring to mind a movie that I saw called *Collateral Beauty*. In the movie, Will Smith's character had lost his daughter to cancer, and it forced him into a dark place. He left his wife and he was also losing the company that he had founded with friends. His life was in a deep downward spiral, and his friends concocted a plan to get him to sell the company. There was a scene near the end of the movie where his wife was sitting in the hospital next to an old woman. As she sat there, the old woman began to ask her questions about why she was there in the hospital. The old woman knew that the mother was facing a loss, and at that moment, she uttered a phrase that has taken me a while to understand.

The old woman told the mother that she shouldn't forget to notice the collateral beauty in the moment of the loss. At that point, I began to ask myself how collateral beauty is possible in loss. There is nothing beautiful about the pain and suffering that one goes through in a time of grief. I dismissed the thought because I figured it was just a movie and maybe the writer just needed some catchy phrase to tie the movie together. However, I couldn't shake the thought of this title and began to ask God to show me the collateral beauty from the death of Kenisha.

I really didn't see how there could be any beauty from her death. The last two years of my life have been everything but beautiful because my anger turned me against everything that I once held dear to my heart. Grief had caused me to feel pain and sorrow, darkness, and loneliness. How could any of that be considered beautiful?

It took time to come to the revelation, and God had to show me how beauty is produced out of destruction, but I am confident that all things work together for His good. The beauty that I have noticed is that my relationship with God is now stronger and more confident. My trust in Him is on a different level, and fear no longer controls me. My compassion for others has increased due to the knowledge that they are not defined by their problems or their deficiencies. There is no longer a need or desire to judge them from my understanding. Furthermore, my preference now is to see them through the eyes of Christ.

This has allowed me to accept people where they are at and only tell them that it's possible to take another path. Life has become a beautiful journey as I seek to please God rather than man. Truly living for God and relying on Him for every need is liberating, and the freedom feels good. Worshipping God is a daily part of my life as I seek to please Him with all that I do. It makes no difference what man thinks of me anymore because their approval of me is no longer valid.

This goes for those in the church, mostly because Christians have a bad habit of appointing themselves as judge and jury over those that they see as wrong. I am reminded that they didn't understand Jesus when He walked amongst men. He was ridiculed for eating with sinners and He was also accused of being in the service of the devil. So if Christ faced this type of persecution, who are we to think that we will not face the same?

Persecution is not popular, and the flesh is inclined to seek validation. But if you remember what the scripture says, we will not put confidence in the flesh. So I say to you, let us love one another and serve out of a pure heart. The world is full of darkness, and many need the light of Christ to show them the way. Some have been so battered and abused by those professing Christ that they have given up on finding God. They are not coming to the church, so we must go to them.

Like Jesus, we must eat with sinners and those that the church has looked down upon for so many years. We must show them the love of God and not the judgment of our own understanding. Jesus knew the sins of the woman who was about to be stoned, yet He did not hold it against her. Instead, He chose to focus on those passing judgment. I believe as He knelt, writing in the sand, He was exposing the hidden sins of the woman's accusers. So please tell me what is greater in the eyes of God? Is it the open sin or is it the hidden sin? Is it easier to save a hypocrite? Or is it easier to show mercy to someone who may know that they need love?

The Pharisee spoke about all the things that he did for God, and in his mind, he felt justified; however, the publican knew that he needed help as he cried out to God for mercy! Which one of these men did God honor? It is time to stop with our judgments and what we feel is right before God. Who are we to know the wisdom of God? God can use anything and anyone to achieve His plan. We must humble ourselves before the mighty hand of the Lord and let Him lead us.

Sometimes, the leading of God will take you into places that you may not want to go. He may send you in the dope house or the strip club, but remember that you are there for His glory. Quit trying to please man and start pleasing God. Yes, God will give beauty for ashes. You may be the beauty that is sent to help someone to rise out of the ashes of their destruction. Christ left it on record. He loved without condition and He did not judge people according to where they were at. He simply looked upon the lost and pointed them in the direction of hope.

We should be mindful of this fact every time we encounter those that are not as fortunate as we are. This world is cold and cruel, and the enemy of Christ wants to deceive as many as He can. There are many that are suffering. Will you be that healing balm that is placed upon their wounds? Or will you be the instrument of evil that seeks to push them further from the light? This is the collateral beauty that has been produced through the loss of my beloved. Can you find the beauty in your loss? It's there, but you may have to search for it.

> But as for you, you meant evil against me; but God meant it for good, in order to bring it about as it is this day, to save many people alive. (Gen. 50:20 ESV)

Rise Up, Mighty Centurion!

But say the word, and my servant shall be healed. For I also am
a man set under authority, having under myself soldiers: and I say
to this one, Go and he goeth; and to another Come, and he cometh;
and to my servant, Do this, and he doeth it.

—Luke 7:7–8 ASV

This passage of scripture has always intrigued me since I was a
young man growing up. My struggles in life and my journey through
the loss of Kenisha have brought me to this point of being qualified to
be called a centurion. A centurion was one who had been battle-test-
ed through many wars and conflicts. The scars he wore on his body
were proof of his many victories over seemingly impossible odds. This
experience earned him the trust of his peers and those above him to
lead men into battle. They were respected for their bravery, courage,
and fearlessness. Oftentimes, they were brought into strategy sessions
when planning attacks during a conflict because the generals trusted
their skills that were born on the battlefield.

In the scriptures, we see that this centurion had a keen understanding of Christ, and he willingly submitted to His authority. Having risen through the ranks of the Roman army gave this man the understanding of the chain of command and how it was vital to submit
to authorities that ruled over him. This was a bold statement at the
time because as a Roman soldier, you were only supposed to submit
to Caesar and no one else. He could have faced great persecution and
even death for his statement about Christ.

I believe that he saw truth in all that Christ did and said. And
since he was a battle-hardened soldier who had witnessed sickness,

death, and darkness, he needed the healing light of Christ in his and the lives of his soldiers. At that moment, we can see the power of true submission at work. The centurion was a great and mighty leader, yet he willingly chose to be an example to his men by showing them who was the true power and authority in the land.

Like him, I am a man under authority. I am submitted to the will and the way of my Lord Jesus Christ. My sword, shield, and my life belong to Him, and I kneel before Him to present myself as a living sacrifice. The fiery trials that I have faced over the years of my life have hardened me for the task at hand. After losing Kenisha, which was the greatest loss of my life, I can boldly say, "What can this world do to me?"

The fear of man has been laid upon the altar because I now walk with the one who holds the power and the keys to my resurrection. Death no longer concerns me because the life of Christ is alive within me. Death cannot consume, it can only transform. For this reason, I can stare death in the face and laugh.

> O death where is your sting? O grave where is your victory? (1 Cor. 15:55)

Through this loss, God has fashioned me to be His warrior, so surrendering to the evil that seeks to destroy me is not an option. My strength comes from Him and the power of His right hand. My mind and my thoughts are directed by His powerful word that He left on record. "I am a man under authority." My sword has been tested and my shield is true. They have been with me all along and have seen me through many battles. They are my trusted friends who are always there when I need them. My sword is fashioned for my hand to wield, and it will not serve another. God Himself has bestowed my weapons upon me, and no man can take them, nor can any demon in hell stand against them.

> I am more than a conqueror
> through Him who loved us. (Rom. 8:37)

My strength is strong and rooted like the mighty palm tree who sinks its roots deep into the soil to anchor itself. The roots search for an anchor in the darkness of the soil, and it will not stop until one is found. Once it locates a rock that is sufficient, it wraps its roots around the rock until you can no longer tell the difference between the rock and the roots. There in the darkness, it found something strong to hold onto and it would not let go.

Likewise, in the darkness of our lives, we must keep searching until we find the Rock to hold onto. That rock is God, and He is everywhere we need Him to be. The palm tree also has the ability to sway and bend in the winds of the storm. When the wind comes, it will sway and bend, but it will never break. No matter how strong the winds are, the palm tree can ride it out. It just bows down to the ground and lets the winds of adversity and destruction rage over it.

The tree may lose a few palm fronds, but it will never lose the battle. It has learned to lay low until the storm has passed, and then once the danger is over, it rises to stand again. Though it may appear to be dead and destroyed, the palm tree will rise again, just like the death of Jesus when all appeared to be lost. Our Lord and Savior was taken low, only to rise again with victory in his hands. During this storm, I have found myself bowed down and holding on for dear life.

The loss of Kenisha was the worst storm that I have ever encountered. The great winds of anger, guilt, pain, loss, and loneliness unleashed their wrath against me. They pummeled my mind, body, and soul with the force of a thousand hurricanes. Like the palm tree, I had to bend and sway to take on the brunt of the storm, but I never broke.

I wish I could say that it was my own strength that got me through, but that would be a foolish statement indeed. No, I had to realize that God was with me all along. He was there in the midst, protecting me and shielding me from the danger of the storm. For in those times of weakness and wanting to give up, God would always send a word via His angels or a friendly soul to help me hold on.

> He sent his word and healed them, and
> delivered them from their destruction.
> (Psalm 107:20 ESV)

So, like the centurion in the Bible who knew that all Christ had to do is speak (send) the word, and his servant was healed, God sent His word to aid me in my time of need. I didn't think that I was listening because the anger within me kept my conscious mind in darkness. However, the words, the prayers, and the compassion of some spoke to the spirit man within me. My soul was fed and nourished by the Word of God so that I would not hunger or thirst again.

Little did I know, but I was wrapping my roots around that solid rock. Now as the winds clear and the sun shines, I can rise to stand again. I may have lost a few leaves and I may have gained a few more scars, but I know that I possess a new strength and new power.

But what has this produced? What am I now qualified and called to do for my Lord? I patiently await my orders. Like a soldier who has been trained for his mission, I now await your command. Yes, I am qualified, and so are you who go through adverse times. If you look at the scriptures, you will notice that God has never called anyone that He did not qualify. You are not ready for the battle until you have been trained. You can't be a general fresh out of boot camp. It takes time and many fights to make you into the warrior that God wants.

We are dealing with a cold and corrupt world that is heavily influenced by the power of the prince of the air. He has set up his strongholds in many earthly kingdoms, and his dark counsel has spread amongst many. The scripture that states that he can deceive the very elect of God has unfortunately come true as I have seen how we, the church, have fallen short.

We are off course and in need of correction. We are teaching and preaching our own gospels and not the true Gospel. We are commanded to make disciples of Jesus, but I have witnessed, on many occasions, that we are making pastors and spiritual leaders into gods. We have become the church of itching ears, seeking out those who make us feel better about ourselves. We flock to the edifices that lift us up to focus on ourselves and our wants while denying the teaching to be keepers of one another. Self-preservation and the pursuit of earthly treasures have consumed us rather than community involvement and lifting up the downtrodden souls.

I speak to the generals from the authority of the scriptures that for some of you, it is time to stop playing games with God's sheep. The jockeying for positions and titles, instead of directing the troops to go out and seek the lost, must cease. Do you really think that God cares about your title more than He cares about saving this lost and dying world? Your title carries no authority or power unless it is given by God. A pastor, bishop, or apostle should seek to be known by their true name, which was given to all by God. That name is servant. It holds more power than any man-made title in the world.

Yes, your title is man-made because you gave it to yourself, and God never conferred it upon you. I, nor does God, care anything about your title in the church because a title does not save anyone nor does it give you any special privileges. When the prophet Balaam struck the donkey for turning away from the angel of the Lord in the road, who was the greatest in that moment? The donkey saw the destruction before the prophet of God because the prophet had disobeyed God.

> And the angel of the Lord said to him, "Why have you struck your donkey these three times? Behold, I have come to oppose you because your way is perverse before me." (Num. 22:32 ESV)

The lowly donkey was the greatest who saved the life of the prophet. To the generals, the Lord says, "Stop beating your donkeys." God has given you servants to assist and protect you, but your sins and lack of humility has beaten many down. God is the one who gives the orders, and all he wants in return is your service and the fruit that it will produce.

Are you serving the flock through sacrificial service? Or are you fleecing the flock for your own selfish gain? You have forsaken the call to worship the creator, choosing instead to worship the created thing. You gather the spoils of the flock into your earthly storehouses, and you forsake the commandment to store up heavenly treasures. If you will not heed the warning that I give, then enjoy your reward here on earth because you will have to face Jesus one day to give an account of why you continued to go astray. It will be up to His grace and mercy to determine your reward or your punishment.

I pray that God will open your eyes like He did for Balaam and allow you to see the error of your ways. Your earthly kingdom is in ruins as you take the sheep down into the pit. Your lust for power and influence has blinded you to the true mission at hand. You were never supposed to build kingdoms here on earth. You were supposed to build the kingdom of heaven. But remember that those who know the voice of the shepherd will not follow you.

That is why the church is lacking and your members are dwindling.

People are tired of the nonsense and all of the self-imposed judgments that have been placed upon them. It is time to get back to serving out of a true and pure heart. It is time to be our brother's keeper. We must show the world what the true love of God is all about. Hear me now, my fellow soldiers, before it is too late. The handwriting is on the wall. Your kingdom has been numbered, and you have been found lacking.

As I stand to survey the land, I see nothing but destruction, chaos, and ruin. The sounds of weeping women and those that have been discouraged fill the atmosphere. As I kneel to the ground to humble myself and pray, I can feel the anointing of the Spirit lifting me to a higher vantage point. From this position, I can clearly see the damage that has been done and the battles that are taking place across the land. Like an eagle soaring through the heavens in search of its prey, my focus is laser sharp. I see that our armies are scattered and lacking true leadership. We have become rogue mercenaries with no focus and no purpose while denying the fact that there is strength in numbers.

Consequently, the spirit of competitiveness has forced us into trying to best one another. This is one of the tricks that the enemy has used to make us turn on one another instead of waging war against the true foe that wants to destroy all that God has ordained. If that wasn't enough, we have been hit with a combination punch of greed and gluttony coming from the pulpit, which has disguised itself in what is known as prosperity.

My men are running scared, taken captive, or just not engaging in futile battles that produce more chaos and confusion. They have given over their power and authority as they cower in pursuits of fleshly entanglements. You have become "treacherous, reckless, swollen with conceit, lovers of pleasure rather than lovers of God" (2 Tim. 3:4 ESV).

You are lazy and without drive as you seek to find the easy way out. The attraction of fantasy rules your mind as you waste away day in and day out in front of the television, playing video games. While you sit there, wasting precious time and brain cells, a world awaits your leadership and authority. A queen awaits her king. What have you become? Your birthright has been sold for a mere pair of panties as you sacrifice your power and authority upon the alter of lust. The only thing that you are good for is sexual fulfillment and serving a woman's carnal desires, which has allowed them to treat you like the dog that you have become.

To this, I say, "*Stand down! Stand down!*" Your lack of understanding has caused this world to be filled with too many single parent households. And worst of all, you have allowed Jezebel to rise and rule the land. The spirit of Ahab is alive and well all across the land. Many men have fallen victim to this weak and spineless spirit. Ahab was no match for Jezebel and her deceptions. His lack of strength angered God to no end.

> And Ahab the son of Omri did evil in the sight of the Lord, more than all who were before him. And as if it had been a light thing for him to walk in the sins of Jeroboam, the son of Nebat, he took for his wife Jezebel, the daughter of Ethbaal king of the Sidonians and went and served Baal and worshiped him. He erected an altar for Baal in the house of Baal, which he built in Samaria. And Ahab made an Asherah. Ahab did more to provoke the Lord, the God of Israel, to anger than all the kings of Israel before him. (1 Kings 16:30–33 ESV)

It is truly sad to see men acting like the coward known as Ahab in this day and age. Jezebel is using her powers of seduction and lust to lull men into her bed of death. Once you are in her clutches, she twists your mind into thinking that all is well with what is being done. But in the background, she is stripping you and robbing you of your power. The lust will ultimately consume you and deceive you into thinking that you are a king, but in reality, you have become a slave to her will. She does not see you as a man because you are nothing but a stray dog, looking for its next meal in the streets. You're on her leash, and she leads you where she wants you to go because you can't escape the carnal hold she has on your mind, body, and soul.

Ahab thought he was the king. However, everyone knew and feared Jezebel. Even the prophets were afraid of her and what she could do to men. Jezebel caused the prophets to cower in caves and run for their lives. She instituted the worship of Baal and built many altars and groves for this pagan god, all while Ahab sat by and watched. Yes, the king of Israel allowed this abomination to take place. Ahab became weak and turned his back on the true God as he sanctioned the worship of idols.

Today, what are the kings sanctioning? We worship and build altars to idols of flesh and carnality. The strip clubs are filled with misguided boys seeking pleasure; however, they fail to realize that they are cutting their own throats. The lands are filled with men who are too weak to lead, so they cower to their women in search of peaceful conflict resolution. Men have been brainwashed by the phrase "Happy wife, happy life," which has put a choke hold on their authority.

Yes, we should seek to please the ones that we love; however, it should not come at the expense of subjugating your manhood. Tell me this, are you a man who leads or a boy who follows? Your women mock you in the streets and lead you around on leashes. They rage against you for the pain that you have caused with your fall from grace. They are now resorting to seeking their own way and making their own decisions because you sold your birthright to Jezebel. You are no longer relevant in their eyes, nor are you needed for anything other than sex.

Women have become drunk with power and authority as they slide further and further into the destructive plan of the enemy. Where are the generals? Where are the captains? Jezebel has quietly waged war on men over the years. Jezebel is calling out to our women and enticing them with her power. Her voice resonates across the land as many seek to join her ranks. Her beauty and the allure of her flesh has captivated the ranks and lulled many to sleep. She stands in the workplace, the churches, and the home, mocking and ridiculing the creation of God.

Her only desire is to bring men down and make them weak and defenseless by appealing to their carnal nature. Her witchcraft has enticed the women to use their bodies as weapons of destruction. Women are arming themselves unknowingly by enhancing their bodies through surgeries and injections. They have resorted to pursuits of bigger breasts and bigger butts to make themselves more attractive to men.

However, woman, you are not aware that this is a part of the plan to destroy men as a whole. You have become a pawn in the war, a weapon of mass destruction as you flaunt your body before the dogs. You are bait on a hook, and those men that bite are not interested in your mind or what you can achieve. They are only interested in using you and your body to fulfill their bottomless desires.

The men you attract are weak representations of the true man. They really aren't men at all because they have never grown up to face responsibility. Most are little boys pretending to be men. They are looking for someone to mother them, instead of looking to be the leaders that they were called to be. Jezebel thrives on this as she seeks her Ahabs across the land that will serve her. Her siren songs beckon to all who will follow her down the path of destruction. For a time, she has been able to deceive many, but her days have been numbered. In the scriptures, we see that God sent a warrior by the name of Jehu to defeat her. I now call for the Jehus to come forth.

Our ladies have been taken captive by the darkness and are no longer our allies. Rather, unknowingly, they have become pawns of the enemy's plan. He has warped their minds to think that they have the control and that it is essential to maintain it. They have taken the role of headship from the man and turned it into something that was never meant to be. I do not blame them for having to step up due to the lack of true leadership within the ranks of men; however, what should have been temporary has now reached epidemic proportions.

Women are left to themselves, and they are going astray and have no desire to come back into agreement. Women have become drunk off the power given to them by weak boys who have never known what being a man is like. They have taken on the mindset that a man is not needed and that his only worth is to supply her with sex or some other form of temporary passion to fill her needs. She has taken on the role of a man and is trying to play the game that he has played on them for many years.

This thought process was never meant to be, and it is producing generation upon generation of single parents, which has altered the family structure in catastrophic proportions. We now have generations of morally bankrupt women and men who are making up the rules as they go along. This was never meant to be because we have always been a society that was rooted in morality and decency. Women have taken the rules and turned them on their head, and what they do not realize is that they are playing right into the enemy's hands. He has tricked them into thinking that they are in control, but in truth, the enemy has been in control all along. His plan was always to destroy what God set in place.

Men have always been the foundation, and where there is no foundation, there can be no structure. Since the days of Adam and Eve, the enemy has always used the power of deception to destroy the family. Unfortunately, the woman was deceived first, and then the man was taken down. This scenario is being played out to this day, and it seems that no one has recognized it. This is not an indictment against women. As a matter of fact, it should be a wake-up call to all women. It is time to stop being a part of the problem and start being part of the solution.

I have witnessed many who have given up on the idea of marriage and family. Many have adopted the views that it's all about what they want in order to feel fulfilled. Most women have replaced men with the pursuit of careers and education while others have now resorted to the companionship of a dog over a man. Also, I see more and more women opting to have children outside of marriage. Some are in hopes that this will make the boy commit to her; however, I have seen many lives shattered by this tactic.

There are too many single mothers raising children by themselves. This was never meant to be, and I know it seems like all is lost, but God will make a way, and His plan will not be defeated.

> I write to you fathers because you know him who is from the beginning. I write unto you young men because you are strong and the word of God abides in you and you have overcome the evil one.

Do not love the world or the things in the world. If anyone loves the world, the love of the Father is not in him. (1 John 2:13–14 ESV)

THE MISSION

We have gotten way off course, and it is time to look at our GPS (God positioning system) for a course correction. Can you hear the Spirit saying, "Recalculating route?" The centurion has surveyed the land and found that the battle has continued for far too long without any end in sight. The calling on my life has been birthed out of the ashes of loss, and it is time to rise.

My wounds run deep and my scars cover my body after the loss of Kenisha. Though death did not take me, I have still felt the pain of its blade sinking deep into my heart. The voice of the evil one has taunted me from the darkness with his incessant calls of defeat. I know all too well the taste of battle and the agony that it can bring. However, I am a man under authority, and I have been trained for such a time as this.

My weapons are true and tested, and they are always at my disposal, giving me the hope that I need. I'm rolling sixty-six books deep with the Spirit of God as my guiding light. My mantle has been fashioned over time and through many battles. Though I am reluctant to lead others, I know that I have been forged in the fire for such a time as this that we are facing.

> But we have this treasure in jars of clay, to show that the surpassing power belongs to God and not us. We are afflicted in every way, but not crushed; perplexed, but not driven to despair; persecuted, but not forsaken; struck down, but not destroyed; always carrying in the body the death of Jesus, so

that the life of Jesus may also be manifested in our bodies. For we who live
are always being given over to death for
Jesus' sake, so that the life of Jesus also
may be manifested in our mortal flesh.
So, death is at work in us, but life in you.
(2 Cor. 4:7–12 ESV)

This is the mission that we must all submit to in this day and age. We are all to be under the authority of Jesus and walk according to His will. Men must live a life of sacrifice and face death head-on so others may live. Men must wear the scars of battle like badges of honor so that the people will see who works in them to bring about the victory.

It is not by my will alone that I stand here before you. I stand because of the one who has brought me through the battle. Jesus is the only one that can give you and I the strength that we need to fight. If He did it for me, then He surely will do it for all those who serve Him and call on His name. Jesus conquered all and was victorious over death. We can rest assured that we have that same victory because we belong to Him.

Hear me, my brothers, as I call out to the mighty men. This is the life that you and I were born for. We are the keepers of our brothers and the protectors of the realm! We have a duty and a responsibility to one another as brothers in arms. And we must understand that not engaging in battle will never negate the call upon our lives.

You were born with purpose. You can no longer cower in the shadows while the war wages over your territory. You can no longer sit by and think that it doesn't concern you. You cannot be like the disci-ples in the Bible that scattered and lost hope when Christ died on the cross. What they didn't understand is that it was all a part of the plan.

A sacrifice had to be made in order to win the war.

Likewise, a sacrifice must be made for you and I to win this war that the enemy wages on us every day. To the men who have gone astray or those that don't consider themselves worthy because of past mistakes, please hear me. Your sufferings and loss are a part of God's plan, and He will use it to bring about His glory. Keep this in mind when you doubt if you are worthy of God's grace because He is using all of your troubles to make you, not break you.

Although you have been dominated and destroyed on different fronts, God is still in the midst, waiting for you to come home. You have not understood the tactics that have been used against you, and now you are walking wounded. You have given into the darkness and all its filth while denying the light within; however, there is light within you, and all is not lost.

Return to the light and embrace your purpose and destiny so that you may know what true fulfillment of purpose is all about. God did not place you on this earth to be a slave to darkness. You are supposed to be kings! Kings that rule well over their kingdoms and care for their families. The enemy has made you believe that you are supposed to be dogs and players that drop their seed anywhere in the street. You are not a dog; you are a man that was formed in the image of the Almighty God! In you lies purpose, vision, and life! Courageous men do not run from the fight; they boldly charge into the fight. You were designed for battle from the beginning of time!

Men have always fought for what they believed in. It is no different in this day and age because the battle is never over until you rest in the grave. A man's life is marked by struggle, loss, and pain. How we handle these battles is what makes us into the mighty warriors that God expects. You were not designed to sit on the sidelines of life.

You were supposed to uphold honor, truth, courage, and chivalry. God ordained you to be the priest, provider, and protector of your home, your wife, and your children. You are supposed to be fathers, husbands, uncles, and big brothers to the masses because men are the foundation and the strength that holds the entire structure together. God calls you a son, and if you are a son of God, you are victorious in all things.

To the legions across the land, it is time to raise the banners and fight once again. Our resources have been scattered for too long. There is strength in numbers, and our forces need to be concentrated to achieve victory. You are no longer casualties of war; you are victorious kings destined to take territories. Your job is to leave legacy and family because as I stated before, it's not about you. It's about those that come after you. The young boys that come after you need to know how to become real men.

The command has been given to take a wife and care for her and protect her with everything you have, including your life. God has called you to rule your bodies as temples dedicated to him. God calls you the head and not the tail because you were designed and fashioned to be leaders in your homes and your communities. The power of vision lies within you, but it is up to you on how you carry out the plan before you. You see, your original nature was to create, protect, and manage. God gave you dominion over the land and everything in it; however, the "Great Fall of Adam" ushered in our slavery to the sin nature and robbed us of our dominion. That dominion is still calling out to men, and it can be reforged.

The key is to remember where you come from and the lineage that is within. You are descendants of strength and perseverance. The ancestral DNA that overcame the Middle Passage, Ellis Island, and every other destruction known to man is holding fast deep down in your souls. That's why you cannot lose and you will never be destroyed.

For the Spirit is the keeper of your path and the shepherd of your soul.

Can you hear him calling? Can you quiet the rage in your soul for a few moments to hear that small still voice calling for you in the midst of the chaos? Your ears have been seared with hot coals and your hearing has been dulled to the cries of the Spirit. The enemy's voice is loud, boisterous, and contentious. His call stirs up the hatred and the rage within that makes you lash out and destroy. But the voice of the Lord is peace to your inner man and capable of beating back the rage.

The voice of God will allow you to let go of the hurt and the pain through the tears that seek to flow from your eyes. You have held on to pain for far too long, and it is time to release it and direct your thoughts to that place of peace. It is time to cry, my brothers. It is time to mourn and weep to release the pain of loss and struggle. Crying is God's way of release, and there is nothing wrong with letting go. Real men cry; weak men hold it in and suffer. Even Jesus wept, and His example showed us that there is nothing wrong with crying.

So let the tears flow and cleanse your souls of all past hurts and pains. It is time to free yourself from the bondage so that you can come back to where you belong. The never-ending love of Jesus wants you to come back. He is waiting for you to take the first step toward Him so that He can lead you into the light. He wants to give you purpose and a bright future.

Jesus knows your pain and all of your disappointments. He seeks to have a conversation with you about all that you have endured. If you will lay it all at His feet and surrender to His way, He will carry you through to the promises that He left in His Word. His promise to never leave us nor forsake us still holds true to this very day. I know that He has been with me, even in the darkest moments of my life. He was there in the valley, and He will be there on the mountain.

On the day that I lost Kenisha, I thought all hope was gone. However, He was there in the midst, holding me together so that I could make it through. Although the pain of loss blinded me to His presence, He was still there, taking all my sorrow each time I railed against Him. He is God and He can take anything that you can give to Him.

At this point, I must pause for a moment because I am reminded of a very important revelation that I received. We must all understand that we all have to go through in order to reach our destination. I have heard the phrase "The only way to is through" time and time again. However, I did not gain the true understanding of this phrase until my loss.

Too many times, we try to seek alternate routes around our situations, our problems, and life. We try to find ways out of the struggles and hard times because we don't like pain and suffering. This response usually leads us down the rabbit hole of bad decisions and poor choices as we defer to our own wisdom and not the wisdom of God. In truth, we only make things worse when we try to go our own way. However, God left it on record that if we allow Him to take us through, He will bring us to victory.

Here are just a few examples to solidify this point. Abraham had to leave his family and all that he knew to get the promises of God. Joseph had to go through being sold into captivity by his brothers. He also had to serve time in prison for a crime that he did not commit. The Israelites had to go through the wilderness for forty years to reach the promised land. Daniel had to go through the furnace and the lion's den. David had to go through Goliath and Saul to be king. Elijah had to go through Jezebel and the prophets of Baal. And, yes, even Jesus had to go through the suffering and mocking of His own people to give us the victory. His road through was the greatest of all because He had to endure the cross for our victory.

So please tell me why we are afraid to go through? We have some of the greatest examples on record of how the disciples endured, but God saw them through it all. God gave them the victory, even though it didn't look like they would be victorious. But therein lies the key to this whole equation. When God is involved, it will always look bleak to our natural eyes because we cannot see what He sees.

Remember the shadow in the valley? Death, pain, and suffering are small objects that appear to be large and formidable. They are using the light to block your view while giving you a false illusion of being so much greater. So don't look at the problem, look at God and follow Him. He will get you through. But in order to do this, we have to stop listening to the world. The world does not seek the things of God, for it does not know God. It is steeped in darkness and it pulls all who worship it down into the pit of depravity and despair.

In this world resides no good thing. This world is cold, cruel, and without love. We are commanded to shun loving the world and earthly treasures, yet we still run after all it has to offer every day. The greed, competitive nature, and hypersexualization of the world fills our hearts and keeps us from serving God. If we are not careful, it will enslave our minds and rule our destinies. If we are not careful of the games that this world plays on us every day, we will continue to slide down the slippery slope of destruction.

While there are many distractions out there, I want to focus on some core attacks that are doing the most harm to men and their destinies. There are four fronts of battle that have overtaken men. Incarceration, extended adolescence, career focus over family, and lack of education. These are the battles that I seek to draw attention to because they all have the same impact of destroying the family. And these fronts attack every man living on the earth today with no regard to race, creed, or socioeconomic background.

If you are a man, the object of the game is to destroy your strength, your power, your leadership and your headship.

Tell me, my brothers in arms, why are we still falling into the system of incarceration? I know that there is a problem out there that seeks to keep us wrapped up in the prison cycle. Unfortunately, the prison system has become the new plantation for so many men. Statistics show that we lead the world in incarceration rates for men. Many of these men are the products of no fathers or viable role models while growing up. We all know that poverty and lack of education are strong contributors to this problem, but I have to say that in this day and age, prison is still a choice that men make. There is no one twisting your arm to make you commit crimes and atrocities against society. You have chosen to go down this road and you have been deceived into thinking that this is some rite of passage that makes you a man.

That is a lie from the pit of hell! You are not a man because you do what's wrong. You are a man because you do what's right. There are far too many brilliant minds that are locked up behind walls that only seek to destroy them. Part of the problem is the fact that you don't know your history because it has been systematically wiped out over time. You have fallen victim to miseducation in school systems that did not seek to educate you in truth. Your history has been white-washed because the darkness does not want you to come into the true understanding of who you really are and what you can produce. You don't know where you come from, and you lack the vision to see where you are going. Caught up in the endless fog and darkness that surrounds you, you have been left to wander aimlessly through the world.

Like me, you have fallen victim to the emotions of anger and rage, which is common amongst men because we seek to destroy what we don't understand. Unfortunately, your mind and heart were not equipped to handle these raw emotions. Your moral compass has been afflicted with the death and destruction that fills your optics on a daily basis.

This altered life has become your norm as death has taken you captive and made you its slave. You embrace death and destruction and esteem its authority because it has you under the delusion that it is powerful. However, you have made a lie into your truth because this is not what God intended for the men that he created. I want men everywhere to know that there is a new normal that needs to be embraced. We have to speak life to dead situations, dreams, and hopes. We have to find solutions to the prison problem because too many good men are going down the wrong path.

Through my travels, I have come to know that most men have stopped trying to be leaders and providers. The term that they have given this phenomenon is known as "extended adolescence," and it has become quite detrimental to our society as a whole. Men are reverting back to boyhood pleasures and not taking responsibility for anything. They are choosing to live with their parents well into adulthood with no care for marriage, family, or taking care of their own homes. They work menial jobs and sit at home, playing video games for hours and hours throughout the day.

This video game obsession has become an epidemic, and it is a tactic that is being used to destroy men. You are weak and cowardly if you prefer to sit in front of a television all day, fantasizing about being a mythical warrior or a soldier battling on some simulated battlefield. Don't you know that there is true battle raging all around you? There are attacks taking place in your communities on a daily basis that need your attention and guidance. You are wasting your life and your precious time.

From my vantage point, I see men who don't want to engage life and all that it has to offer. I am not sure why, but we need to find out what makes you crave fantasy over reality. The video games have become your drug of choice to suppress your thoughts and emotions. It has become your shield that blocks the pain that you don't want to feel.

I know that it seems easier to hide in your fantasy world for hours and hours, but the problems still remain. Life is still happening all around you, and you are missing out on a fantastic journey. Instead of pretending to be a soldier, how about stepping up and becoming a real soldier of purpose? A soldier that doesn't destroy life but gives life to others? There are people out there that need what you have to offer. How long will you sleep on your gift? How long will you trade your precious time for worthless fantasies? You were not designed to be a child all of your life.

> When I was a child, I spoke like a child,
> I thought like a child, I reasoned like a
> child. When I became a man, I gave up
> childish ways. (1 Cor. 13:11 ESV)

In the old days, we called it a "rite of passage," which was a time when a boy was taken from his mother to go with the men of the tribe. The boy was shown how to be a man by being with men and seeing them in action. We have lost this valuable rite over time, and now we find our young men hanging on to childish ways and not understanding how to become men.

Career-focused men are very detrimental to the plan of God. Hear me when I say this, my brothers. It is not wrong to pursue a career and be excellent at what you do. God would not have it any other way. However, it is wrong to focus solely on your career and the pursuit of all it will bring while neglecting your family and personal lives. I am tired of hearing men saying that they can't focus on finding a woman because they have to get their lives together first. They give excuses like, "I need to get my finances together," "I need to be able to provide for a woman," or "I'm waiting on God to direct me to my queen." This is nothing more than a diversionary tactic, and it is time to put it to rest. Truth is, you will never get your life together until you do what God is telling you to do.

> Therefore a man shall leave his father
> and his mother and hold fast to his
> wife, and they shall become one flesh.
> (Gen. 2:24 ESV)

God has given men a commandment to seek wives, not whores, whose only goal in life is to rob you of your manhood. God never commanded us to go out and make bastards either, and it is time to stop being stray dogs who drop their seed in the streets. A wife was designed for you to help you and to make you the best man that you can be. With her by your side, you will be able to get yourself together because she wants the best for you.

Your career will not be all that you want it to be without her because your work is in vain. You need a good woman behind you, motivating you to be the best that you can be. You need her strength, her nurturing, and her loving care when times get rough. She is more than a pair of panties that only supply temporary release.

God has designed a woman who will be the protector of your heart and emotions. She will be there to soothe you and love you through the good and the bad. My brothers, this is the life that God wants for all who seek to follow Him. Don't get me wrong. You can be successful without your wife, but you will never be what God wants you to be, which is a husband, a provider, and the extension of His hand on the earth. Stop making excuses and start taking action.

Men are to pursue and not wait. A wolf does not sit and wait for what he hunts. Rather, he catches the scent and pursues his prey. God has given us the natural ability to hunt and gather since the beginning of time. Unfortunately, we have been hunting the wrong things. Women are not to be preyed upon for sport. Most men have likened this to sport fishing by thinking that they can catch and release. This has caused a whole host of problems over the years, and it is getting worse.

When I was growing up, the old-timers called it "sowing your oats," which was accepted across the board by everyone. But there comes a time when you have to leave childish things behind and grow up. I look back on that wisdom now and wish that I could go back and talk to myself. I would warn the young me about the dangers and pitfalls that I would face in the future because of my careless ways. Although I am not able to go back in time, I hope that these words are resonating in some man's ears right now.

Stop your foolishness! God's word is still true and it still stands to this day. My brothers, it is time to grow up and take wives. It is time to take a stand and show the women of this world what true men are all about. I firmly believe that if we stand up as men, then the women will gain respect for us and, in turn, get their acts together. We must be the leaders because we must be the ones who bring light into the darkness.

The light that I speak of is the light of knowledge and education, which are keys to victory if we want to win the war that is being waged on men. Since when did the pursuit of stupidity become a badge of honor? Education is power, and it has the ability to knock down any barrier that stands in front of you. An educated man is a threat while ignorance ensures destruction. We must challenge our men to pursue the excellence of education.

Education can never be taken away from you. Knowledge is more precious than riches and material things. It can come in many forms, not just college and academia because I believe that not everyone is destined for college. It would be nice if we all possessed degrees from institutions of higher learning; however, there is great worth in obtaining vocational training in the skilled labor arena.

I remember my father telling me that everyone has their place in life. For every person that wants to be a doctor, there are those that only seek to be a janitor. Each one has a role in life, which is equally important. You wouldn't want to go to a filthy doctor's office, would you? So let us give due respect to all who seek out honest work.

My grandfather's name was Leo Page, and he was a great man in my eyes. Growing up, I honored and respected him for all of his accomplishments during his life. My grandfather migrated to Detroit from the south to work in an auto factory at a young age. He was a hard worker who understood his role in life. He accepted his role as husband, father, and provider without any hesitation. In spite of all of the obstacles and limitations that he faced, he found a way to provide for his wife and thirteen children without sacrificing his integrity or doing damage to his character.

He never graduated from high school or college, but my grandfather was one of the smartest men that walked the earth. He knew how to do electrical work, build houses, lay cement, and work on cars. One day, I had the chance to ask him how he became so educated without going to school. As we stood there in the midst of his vegetable garden, which was his pride and joy, he told me the secret that I will never forget. He said, "Knowledge is free, and everything you need to know can be found in books."

He went on to say that the library is the greatest resource to all of us because it is a wealth of information. My grandfather lived a life of excellence because he never ceased to educate himself on the things that he needed to know. He didn't let his lack of a diploma or a degree stop him. He found a way to overcome by seeking knowledge.

As men, we must also seek knowledge and never let our circumstances dictate our direction. We have been denied education for far too long. It is time for us to learn about ourselves, our history, and the history of our accomplishments in society. We will never truly understand where we are going until we learn where we have come from. History records itself as a guide to aid us so that we do not repeat the same mistakes, but it also can be a source of pride in knowing that our ancestors faced overwhelming odds but still managed to succeed.

We will never be the men that we should be as long as our minds are enslaved by ignorance. Knowledge and education are powerful weapons in the hands of a man. Will you seek that power? Or will you continue to bow down to death and destruction?

The war that has been waged on us is using the age-old strategy of divide and conquer. Our forces are scattered across the land. We are not being as effective as we could be if we were to join forces and fight together for the common good. I know that there are groups of men out there who are doing the work. You have been successful on some fronts, but how much more successful could we be if we joined together across the land?

We all seek the same, which is to raise strong men. We should not fight against each other for the same goal. The strategy to divide and conquer has worked, and many men are walking wounded instead of in victory. I call to my men in arms! Stand with me once again and prepare for battle! The war for the kingdom is still at hand, and all is not lost. Sin abounds across the land, but grace abounds much more.

I call to the warriors and to the mighty men of valor! Reform the ranks and strengthen yourselves for the fight of your lives. You were called to serve, and you have taken oaths to defend the will of God! It is time to fulfill your oaths and walk in victory because you cannot be defeated. In you lies the Spirit of God like a burning ember that seeks to reignite! All it requires is a fresh supply of oxygen to make you burn once again. You need a fresh wind that can only come from the Spirit of God. Ask God to breath on you once again and give life to every situation in your life. Reform the ranks and take your place beside me! We have a charge to keep, we have a God to serve, and we can take the land and reclaim our standing.

I call to the generals. It is time to repent and recalculate your route! God is a loving and forgiving God, and He wants you to know that. The generals must get back to the mission of preparing the people for the eternal and not the world. It is time to build treasures in heaven because this life is only temporary. We were made to serve God and not ourselves. It is time to lay down egos and vanity so that we can join to fight our common enemy.

To the generals, I say you cannot deny the men! Men have always been the key in this battle because we are the foundation in which everything else is built. Over time, the enemy has weakened the foundation through various battles, but he is never able to destroy that which God has made.

We must lay the chief cornerstone in the lives of men and get them to understand who they belong to. We must preach Jesus to the men across the land. They must understand that Jesus was the ultimate man's man. He is the true representation of what we are to be in this life and the life after. We must teach that we were made to care and take responsibility for those around us.

I call to the Jehus that will defeat and slay the Jezebels across the land. Jezebel, I decree that your reign is over, and you will be trampled under the feet of my mighty men! I call to the true men of valor who serve God with a pure heart. It is time to wipe the house of Ahab from the earth! For all those who follow after the spirit of Ahab, your days are numbered. We will not allow any friends, priests, or great men who identify with this spirit to go forth any longer. We are the true men, and we will not bow down to worthless idols controlling women or ungodly ideals.

To my ladies in waiting, I speak this commandment and ask that you heed my words. You were made to birth in the natural and in the spiritual. You have the ability to birth purpose and life. The power of life and death resides within you. Will you use what you have been given to birth construction instead of destruction? You were meant to be a partner and not a lone rogue. It is not in your DNA to be single, no matter how comfortable it may feel. You were made to share and to care. God fashioned you to be the emotional seat of a man and to be his balance.

Likewise, the man was made to balance your emotions, but the enemy has confused you and gotten you to become rooted in conflict rather than resolution. You have taken power, but you are out of balance, and this world needs you to be in harmony as God created you to be.

Women, hear me when I say this. It's time for a route recalculation. I know that you have been hurt for far too long. I have seen your pain and know the intimacy of your grief. I have sat by and watched your frustration grow over the lack of good men. And even now, I see how you have abandoned your hope and resorted to following your own way.

Please know that your current course is leading you down the wrong path. You are off course and in danger of losing out on the blessings that God has prepared for you. I really need you to help me in this fight because you are one of the keys to our victory. It will require work and effort, which is something that I know you can do. But you have to put down the hurt and pain first. The only way to do this is to go to the one who can take all of the pain away. Jesus is there, waiting for you to drop your walls and be honest. Give him your worst emotions because Jesus can take anything you can dish out. Trust me on this one, ladies because I've said some things to Him that I will never repeat to anyone. His grace is sufficient for anything we throw at Him. Just know that I want all women to know and have the love that I had for my beloved Kenisha. It is possible, but you have to be willing to follow the right map.

ATTACK!

Now that we understand the mission, it is time to execute the attack strategy. Fear not. You are destined to conquer all that comes against you, and it is time to rise up! It is time to be the men you were called to be. God knows your path and the plan that He has set for your life. It is up to you to engage God and get in the battle. If you are still doubting whether or not your strength matters, take a look around your home and your community. Don't you want to see change? Or are you just accepting that this is just the way it is? Do you care about the future and the future of your children? If so, then please stand up and stand with me.

We have seen the problems and all the destruction, and now it is time to work on the solutions. We must say to ourselves, "Yes, I am my brother's keeper. I care about those around me and I want to see all men succeed." This is the mindset and mentality that we must adopt. True, we have been mistreated, abused, robbed, and left for dead. However, I am reminded of King David who was one of the greatest warriors in the Bible. In the book of 1 Samuel we see that upon returning to Ziklag, David and his men discover that the enemy has invaded and taken their families captive. Ziklag was burned to the ground, and all of its inhabitants were enslaved but not killed.

David and his men were so overcome with grief that they wept until they could weep no more. Bitterness and anger swept through them, and they even thought of killing David because they all sought to blame him because he was in charge. However, David was a true man, and when he was faced with adversity, he knew where to turn. He knew that his help, his strength, and his wisdom came from God. No matter what the circumstances looked like, he knew that God had the answer.

Yes, the grief and the loss was overwhelming, and it could have destroyed him and all of the mighty men; but in that tense moment, the glory of God was revealed unto all. David, being under great duress, consulted God for instruction. He was a king who was in charge, but he recognized someone greater than himself. He knew that he was a man under authority, so he humbled himself before God and all of his men.

> And David inquired of the Lord, Shall I pursue after this band? Shall I overtake them? He answered him, pursue, for you shall surely overtake and shall surely rescue. (1 Sam. 30:8 ESV)

Men, we must humble ourselves and consult the one true God because He is the ultimate authority over our existence. We have tried to go about this on our own and have produced nothing. We have been slaughtered on the battlefield for far too long. Yes, it is time to pursue and take back what has been stolen. However, we must consult the Lord to give us instructions on how to recover that which was lost and taken. We have wept for far too long. The bitterness and anger have become cancerous to our souls, which has caused us to turn on one another.

We must first pursue unity and break down the walls of division that exist between us. It is time to bury the past sorrows and look forward to our future joy. The time has come to pursue love, not hate; to pursue our wives and our families, not whores and riches. It is time to pursue our queens and bring them home to the palace that they deserve. You are kings that are worthy of kingdoms and land. It is time to pursue knowledge, not ignorance.

There should be no shame in our men that seek to educate themselves. Education is worthy of the highest honor because it brings about excellence and not insufficiency. It is time to pursue God and not the world because there is nothing that is good in this world. This world will pass away, but God and His kingdom are eternal. This life is about choices, and your choices have consequences.

You can choose to live in lack and depravity or you can live in victory. You can leave your mark upon the world or you can die without mention or notice. The choice is yours. God wants you to choose a life that is poured out in ways that will heal, build, and love others. Let us be warriors of construction instead of slaves to destruction. Though we live in trying times, though we dwell in foreign lands that are not our own, God has left us an eternal promise that we will flourish.

> Thus, says the Lord of host, the God of Israel, to all who were carried away captive, whom I have caused to be carried away from Jerusalem to Babylon: Build houses and dwell in them; plant gardens and eat their fruit. Take wives and beget sons and daughters; and take wives for your sons and give your daughter to husbands, so that they may bear sons and daughters. That you may be increased there, and not diminished. (Jer. 29:4–7 ESV)

THE CONCLUSION
OF THE MATTER

I, the centurion, write this to my mighty men of valor! You can rise out of your sorrow and be victorious. We have all suffered loss, pain, and rejection, but I need you to look at it from another perspective. Whatever you have gone through is not meant to hold you down; rather, it is meant to lift you up. You were born for such a time as this, and you can make it.

Take a look at my journey and know that you can be victorious. I have stared death in the face, and it has taken everything from me that was once my world. But God was there to bring me through the worst time in my life. If I can live to stand and fight again, then so can you. Yes, it was and still is painful, but the pain is different now and is forcing me to see the truth of this world. The pain is there to let me know that we do not belong to ourselves. We don't have the power that we think we have. The pain has actually revealed the true path that we all must walk.

This is what it means when I say that we are going from grief to glory because God is the only one that can take pain and suffering and turn it into power and purpose. This is the mystery that I speak of when Paul asked God to remove that thorn from his side, and God told him all he needed was grace. That grace that God gives is the true glory of His omnipotence. If we say that we will submit to the authority and will of God, then we must be willing to accept and bear the cross that comes with it. However, we must also understand that our cross comes with a promise.

The scripture states that we are to become heirs with Christ, which means that we are adopted sons into the kingdom of God. This adoption comes at a great cost to us because Christ had to suffer the worst death known to man to bring us back into the kingdom.

> Surely he has borne our griefs and carried our sorrows; yet we esteemed him stricken, smitten by God, and afflicted, But he was pierced for our transgressions; he was crushed for our iniquities; upon him was the chastisement that brought us peace and with his wounds we are healed. All we like sheep have gone astray; we have turned, every one, to his own way; and the Lord has laid on the iniquity of us all. (Isa. 53:4–6 ESV)

Christ gave it all and paid it all so that we would not have to suffer. But I know what you are thinking. You are suffering right now because of a loss, a setback, or some horrible mistake. So how is it that this is still taking place, even though the Bible says that Christ paid it all?

The answer is quite simple. There is no gain without pain and suffering, and therein lies the problem because no one wants to suffer. But if you really think about it, in the natural, we will endure the pain of the gym in order to get that ripped muscular body. Women will endure the pain of childbirth to bring that beautiful child into the world. Childbirth is no laughing matter, and I have witnessed what a woman endures in that process. All I can say is that I'm glad I'm a man because the pain a woman experiences looks to be very intense. But you go through it because of the joy that is felt when the pain and suffering is over. Pain is a natural part of life, and I believe that God allowed it because it is a gateway to joy and glory.

> For I consider that the sufferings of this present time are not worth comparing with the glory that is to be revealed to us. For the creation waits with eager longing for the revealing of the sons of God. (Rom. 8:18–19 ESV)

God has promised us that we will experience glory and joy after the suffering. But please tell me why we don't want to endure the suffering for Christ who has promised us eternity? This world and everything that is in it is temporary. After this life on earth, we all have an eternal resting place that is predicated upon what we do in this life.

I don't know about you, but I have experienced great suffering here and do not wish to continue it in eternity. I would rather suffer temporarily so that I can receive the future promise of eternal glory with God. This is the mystery of pain and loss because we think of them as harmful in the natural; however, they can be quite beneficial to us. My mind is strengthened and my heart is sure. I know that one day, I will see all those who have gone on before me, including my beloved Kenisha. But until then, I have a duty and a mission to perform here. We as men are all charged with a duty to serve.

> Fear God and keep his commandments, for this is the whole duty of man. (Eccl. 12:13 ESV)

My duty is to preach and teach the love of God to all those that are in need. It is as if the pain and the loss have motivated me more. In this war, we will lose many to the forces of darkness, but we will not leave anyone on the battlefield. Everyone who fights in the name of the Lord will make it home to receive the honor that they are due. When that day comes, I want all of us to be able to say, "I have fought the good fight, I have finished the race, I have kept the faith, Henceforth there is laid up for me the crown of righteousness, which the Lord, the righteous judge will award to me on that day, and not only to me but also to all who have loved his appearing" (2 Tim. 4:7 ESV).

Until that day comes, we will continue to wear our battle scars as a testimony of our struggles and how we made it through. The scars will tell a story to all those who look upon you and wonder if they can make it. Let your fight be a legacy that will be remembered through the generations so that your name will live on throughout time. This is the way of the warrior and the path for all who choose to fight.

We can no longer sit on the sidelines and watch as our women and children suffer. We must be their covering and their guide. It is my sincere hope and prayer that you will hear my words and join me in this fight. I need more mighty men to battle the forces that are coming against us, and I cannot do it alone. We can become a mighty army in the name of the Lord if we will only turn to him and give him our pain.

Just know that you're suffering for a reason that is greater than you. Your grief can take you to glory so that one day, you can know that the fight was worth the struggle. I leave you with this quote from Robert Downey Jr., who has faced many struggles that have brought him to triumph. This man is a true soldier and worthy of honor. "People rise out of the ashes because they are invested in the possibility of triumph over seemingly impossible odds." No truer words have ever been spoken.

May God speak to the hearts of everyone who reads my words.

In Jesus's name. Amen.

About the Author

Eric Lomax has served many ministries and denominations for over twenty-five years. He entered ministerial training in 1995 at Allen Temple Baptist Church under Pastor J. Alfred Smith Sr. He was ordained as an elder in the Great Lakes First Ecclesiastical Jurisdiction COGIC under the late Bishop Walter E. Bogan in August of 2000. He has served as a superintendent of Sunday school, associate pastor, and as an adjutant to the late Bishop Benjamin Gibert at Detroit World Outreach church. While at DWO, he also served with his late wife, Kenisha V. Lomax, on the Prayer Engine Team, Song of Solomon Marriage Ministry, and the Men of Valor men's ministry.

Eric is a man on a mission! He wants to see men fulfill their true purpose and God-given potential. He has the true heart of a servant, especially for men who have strayed away from the church or those struggling to understand their role in the kingdom. He has launched Centurion Ministries, which seeks to empower men to be all that God wants them to be.

Thanks to the help of David Kessler and his grief support group, Eric has come to understand that the grieving process is an intricate web that many can become tangled in. Men are particularly vulnerable and can become lost in a raging river of emotions. Eric seeks to offer hope to those men who are struggling to navigate the difficulties that they face after suffering a loss.

Eric currently lives in Detroit, Michigan, with his wife, Candice, and his daughter, Tristan. They attend Oak Pointe Church in Novi, Michigan, under Pastor Bob Shirock. He continues to serve and speak to groups of men to show them that God is there when you need Him.

9 781647 731625